Water management in industrialised riverbasins

ORGANISATION FOR ECONOMIC CO-OPERATION AND DEVELOPMENT
PARIS 1980

The Organisation for Economic Co-operation and Development (OECD) was set up under a Convention signed in Paris on 14th December 1960, which provides that the OECD
shall promote policies designed:
- to achieve the highest sustainable economic growth and employment and a rising
  standard of living in Member countries, while maintaining financial stability, and
  thus to contribute to the development of the world economy;
- to contribute to sound economic expansion in Member as well as non-member
  countries in the process of economic development;
- to contribute to the expansion of world trade on a multilateral, non-discriminatory
  basis in accordance with international obligations.

The Members of OECD are Australia, Austria, Belgium, Canada, Denmark, Finland,
France, the Federal Republic of Germany, Greece, Iceland, Ireland, Italy, Japan, Lux-
embourg, the Netherlands, New Zealand, Norway, Portugal, Spain, Sweden, Switzerland,
Turkey, the United Kingdom and the United States.

∴

TABLE OF CONTENTS

This report has been prepared on the basis of seven case studies provided by seven Member countries (Australia, France, Japan, the Netherlands, Sweden, United Kingdom, United States) in the framework of the OECD Water Management Group. The seven countries directly concerned actively participated in this programme in preparing the detailed outline of the report, in providing the case studies and performing a detailed review of a first draft of the present report which has been written with the help of Messrs. B.T. Bower and P.F. Ténière-Buchot.

This study is the follow-up of the report on Water Management Policies and Instruments published by the OECD in 1977.

Two characteristics are common to the two studies:

- The topics studied: management of water quality and quantity, the administrative organisations, the legal and economic instruments available, the achieved results.
- The countries reviewed: Canada, Finland, France, Japan, the Netherlands, Germany, United Kingdom, United States, in the case of the 1977 report. Australia, France, Japan, the Netherlands, United Kingdom, Sweden, United States, in the case of the present study; thus, five countries are common to both studies. However, the present study focusses on specific river basins.

It is thus advisable to refer to the 1977 report on Water Management Policies and Instruments which, in a sense, is an introduction to this in-depth study based on seven very detailed national case studies.

SUMMARY

The seven river basins representing the case studies in seven Member countries (Australia, France, Japan, the Netherlands, Sweden, United Kingdom, United States) reflect differences in degree of urbanisation and industrialisation; geographical size; hydrology; complexity and seriousness of water management problems; and governmental or organisation for water resources management. Despite these differences, there are some commonalities in the approaches to water management which are reflected in the synthesis report, and in this summary.

Ambient water quality standards

The primary focus of the case studies was water quality management. In carrying out water quality management, all of the countries represented by the case studies, except Australia and Sweden, have established ambient water quality standards which are to be achieved and maintained. These standards are comprised of 10-20 indicators of water quality. The case studies show that ambient water quality standards:

a) may be differentiated in a river basin among river reaches and water bodies, including within the same river, to take into account varying uses of water within a basin;

b) may be varied by time of year, for example, to require higher standards during periods of fish migrations;

c) are dynamic in the sense that new standards may be added and existing ones modified as new information on and knowledge of effects are obtained;

d) are rarely specified in terms of probability to reflect the stochastic (basically random) nature of discharges and of water availability; and

e) are established by different levels of government or combination of levels in the different countries.

Implicitly in Australia and Sweden, and explicitly in the other five countries, the quantitative ambient water quality standards are the stimuli for water quality management. That is, various governmental programmes are adopted and private entities are induced to take actions, all with the objective of achieving and maintaining the

9

ambient standards. These standards are to be met by imposing on individual and collective activities which discharge to water bodies:
(1) discharge standards and best management practices; or (2) discharge standards, best management practices, and effluent charges.
Standards may specify inputs, production processes, product specifications, maximum quantities of residuals which can be discharged each
day, various combinations of these. Charges may be imposed on discharges into collective (municipal) sewage treatment plants as well
as on discharges directly to water bodies. Combinations of discharge
standards and effluent or user charges are possible.

Financing water quality management

The case studies show clearly the importance of distinguishing
operationally between effluent charges and user charges. The former
represent the amounts paid for discharges made directly to water
bodies. User charges are the amounts paid for services, e.g., treatment in a municipal sewage treatment plant of the discharges from an
individual activity. Both types of charges are levied per unit of
discharge. (Pollution charges are comprised of user charges and
effluent charges.)

The purpose of all user charges systems and of all effluent
charge systems currently in existence is to raise revenues to finance
public and private facilities for improving water quality, such as
treatment plants and reservoirs, and the associated administrative
activities. Whether or not such charges act as incentives to induce
activities to reduce discharges, either into water bodies or into
sewage treatment plants, depends on the magnitudes of the charges and
the substitution possibilities available to the individual activity.
Depending on their structure, charges may be equitable, efficient,
either, or both.

All countries impose some form of pollution charges - user
charges, effluent charges, both - on at least some types of activities. However:

1. The procedures for computing charges vary significantly from
   country to country;
2. The proportion of total water quality management costs
   covered by user charges and effluent charges, versus the proportion from other sources of revenue, e.g., general revenue
   sources of governments, varies from country to country, and
   in the United States at least, within the country;
3. The extent of subsidy provided to private and public entities
   for construction of facilities to reduce discharges varies
   substantially from country to country; and,

4. The charges paid by, and the subsidies provided to, an individual activity may result in that the discharger is paying less or more than the share of the water quality management costs attributable to his pollution load (who is subsidising whom?).

Some revenues for water resources management are generated by abstraction fees. However, some types of activities are exempted, and the fees may or may not be significant sources of revenue. As with pollution charges, only if abstraction fees are sufficiently high, will they act as incentives to induce activities to reduce abstractions or modify the origin of abstractions (superficial vs. underground water).

Administrative procedures

Licences are required in most of the countries for withdrawing water from water bodies, except from groundwater in Japan. Permits are required for discharging into water bodies. In both cases certain activities are exempted. Licences and permits, along with monitoring of abstractions, discharges, and ambient water quality are part of the means by which the performance of water quality management programmes are assessed.

User and public participation

The report distinguishes between formal participation (based on laws and regulations) and informal or spontaneous participation (by a wide variety of private interest groups among the public). In both cases, participation in river management decisions is accepted everywhere and even solicited. The means usually employed include meetings of users in consultative assemblies, hearings and public inquiries, and information campaigns. Anglers' and local residents' associations are certainly among the most active participants. As a rule, the level of active participation by users (the aim being to solve water problems) would seem to depend on the degree of user satisfaction. Application of the regulations through legal proceedings and sanctions is always the exception.

Realisation of management objectives

There are five criteria for evaluating the results of water management:

- compliance with pre-established standards indicating the ambient quality of waters;
- the degree of pollution abatement achieved in discharges into natural waters;

- the proportion of pollutant discharges which comply with pre-scribed effluent standards;
- the actual extent to which a financial programme of water investment expenditure planned during a certain period is carried out;
- evaluation of the benefits resulting from improved water quality and availability.

The assumption in such evaluations is that the kind and extent of changes in water quality and polluting discharges can be measured. It should also be possible to monitor implementation of the financial programmes and estimate the benefits by the policy adopted. The many indicators, their variability over time and the effect of non-water management factors make such measurement difficult.

The link between investment expenditure and results affecting the natural environment is often tenuous, since the degree of efficiency in operating facilities and any qualitative changes which may take place in industrial processes are not taken into account. In evaluating the benefits provided by a water policy, systems of preference and social values must lastly be considered.

Water management policy at the river basin level

Some general considerations emerge from this study:
- there are several typical stages when introducing a water management policy in an industrialised basin. The aim, first, is to increase the quantity of dissolved oxygen in surface waters, next to control pollution from non-point sources and allow for a greater variety of pollution parameters, and finally to respect the integrity of the aquatic ecosystem;
- in each case, it is necessary to decide whether it will be more costly to try and solve water pollution problems by technological means or to control industrial settlement by land-use planning. A combined approach is of course possible in the event of limited technical and financial resources;
- there is a tendency to combine the management of surface water and groundwater, both as regards quantity and quality, including the technical, financial and administrative organisation aspects;
- in compliance with current legislation, any disputes between users and the administration are usually settled by seeking a consensus through user participation in the implementation of water policy;
- some of the most urgent problems yet to be solved include the growing difficulty of controlling watercourses, learning more about the mechanisms of watercourse pollution and treatment (micro-pollutants, non-point pollution) what to do with sludge and the ultimate stages of sewage treatment.

Chapter I

BACKGROUND

1. Purpose of Study

The purpose of the study whose results are described in this report was to compare, and evaluate to the extent possible, water resources management in industralised river basins in several OECD Member countries. It was hoped that both the commonalities and differences identified would be useful to Member countries in performing the continuous task of water resources management.

The study procedure was for each participating country to select a single river basin for analysis as a case study. No attempt was made to define criteria which could be applied to select a "representative" river basin. Variation in socio-economic characteristics and hydrologic/geologic characteristics are likely to be large even within a small country. However, what can be representative or typical for a given country is the organisational structure for water resources management. For example, in France, England and Wales, and Sweden, organisational structure is the same throughout the respective countries, along river basin boundaries in the first two, at the national level in Sweden. Hence, the river basins chosen for case studies in those countries are typical, with respect to organisation. In contrast, the river basin selected for the United States (U.S.) case study has an organisational structure which is not typical for the country, there being only one other agency analogous to the Delaware River Basin Commission, the Susquehanna River Basin Commission in the river basin adjacent to the Delaware on the west.

This synthesis report is based on the seven case studies submitted. These case studies in turn were based on an extensive set of questions developed by the Steering Committee of the project. Because the seven countries involved had varying degrees and types of water quality problems and different administrative structures, not all questions were relevant to each country. Further, more data were available in some countries and on some questions than in other countries and on other questions. The synthesis report attempts to reflect and emphasize the useful data available in the case studies.

2. Focus of Study

Water resources management is comprised of the totality of tasks required to produce water and water-related goods and services. Water resources management is a production function which transforms the quantity, quality, time, and location characteristics of surface and ground water resources into the quantity, quality, time, and location characteristics of the desired outputs: irrigation water, hydro-electric energy, water-based recreation opportunities, flood damage reduction, municipal water, industrial water, navigation opportunities, fish biomass, water quality. The characteristics of water and water resources systems define the physical-technological-biological context of water resources management. Related to this context and interrelated among themselves, as shown in Figure I-1 are: 1) the system outputs; 2) the management tasks; 3) the level of government performing each task for each output; and 4) time. The demand for any output, the tasks relating to the output, and the level of performance of the tasks all may be both stochastic and change over time.

Figure 1-1

COMPONENTS OF WATER RESOURCES MANAGEMENT
COMPOSANTES DE LA GESTION DES RESSOURCES EN EAUX

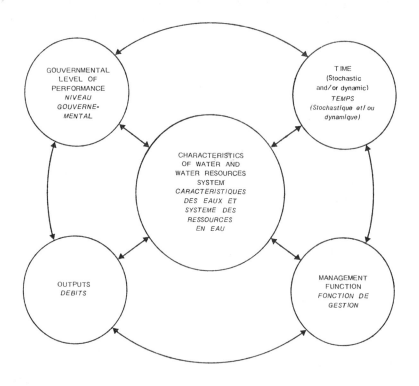

To produce the desired outputs from a water resources system a set of tasks must be performed. These tasks include: data collection; research; analysis; planning; design; construction; operation and maintenance of facilities; forecasting quantity and quality of streamflows; forecasting quality of lakes and ground water bodies; monitoring water withdrawals, wastewater and residuals discharges,

and ambient water quality; inspecting facilities; setting of regulations, standards, charges, constraints on withdrawals and discharges;
setting of regulations, standards, constraints on production processes
and products; collecting fees/charges; mapping flood plains; operating flood warning networks, and evacuating people and goods when necessary; imposing sanctions (enforcement) for non-compliance with
standards/regulations/procedures.

In all countries, even where integrated water resources management agencies exist - integrated in the sense of having responsibility
for the entire production function - multiple "actors" are involved,
if not in the provision of water and water-related products and services, then in the use of those outputs. The actors include the
governments of general jurisdiction which decide who gets what, when,
where, how, for example, what water quality level, how much water at
what cost, how much subsidy for installation and/or operation of waste
treatment facilities.

Within this broad context, the study reported herein focussed on
two aspects of water resources management: 1) water quality management; and 2) management of withdrawals of water from surface and
ground water sources. The implications, for both these aspects, of
river regulation for hydroelectric generation, of dredging and chan-
nelisation, of irrigation return flows, are not explicitly addressed.

3. Some Universal Facts of Life with Respect to Water Resource Management

It is important to emphasize certain basic "facts of life" which
underlie, in particular, the water quality management component of
water resources management.

1) No activity - manufacturing process, residential activity,
agricultural operation - transforms 100 per cent of inputs into desired products and services. There is always something "leftover",
a residual which must be disposed of in some manner. Most often disposal is to one or more of the environmental media: water, air,
land.

2) Until relatively recently, use of the environment for the disposal of residuals was free. Similarly, there was no charge for withdrawing water from water bodies. Consequently, a rational plant
manager, individual farmer, store owner, householder, used as much
of those inexpensive factor inputs as possible in producing his goods
or services. Such behaviour led to an excessive use of the common
property resources.

3) In all countries there is increasing pressure on the finite
water resource, as a result of increasing withdrawals and increasing
discharges. As demands grow in relation to supply - as appears likely
with increasing population and/or production of goods and services

and without a major change in life style - the increased demands will result in increased patterns of interaction among users and in increased incidence of conflicts. Because the assimilative capacity of the environment is essentially fixed, ignoring long-run climatic changes, that capacity will only become more scarce in the future relative to the demands on it. Inevitably then, the price on its use will increase, just as for any increasingly scarce resource. This is true no matter how the price is reflected, that is, in withdrawal changes, effluent standards, input constraints, product restrictions, effluent charges, or some combination.

4) Water resources management must be carried out with explicit consideration of air and land resources, because all forms of residuals and the three environmental media are interrelated. One form of residual can be transformed into another. If undesirable materials or energy are removed from a liquid discharge stream, they must go either to the air or to the land, or into the water as another type of liquid residual. Similarly, if constraints imposed on the discharge of gaseous residuals to the atmosphere result in the application of a wet scrubbing system, a liquid effluent results which requires disposal. Sludge from sewage treatment plants is another example of these interrelationships.

5) The removal of materials and/or energy from a liquid or a gaseous discharge stream requires the addition of materials and energy. These added materials and energy virtually always become residuals. Thus, "conventional waste treatment" increases the total quantity of residuals for disposal. Such treatment is applied because it is assumed that the "secondary" residuals generated in the treatment have less adverse effects when discharged than the original residual (pollutant).

6) Water resources management takes place in a dynamic context. In all societies there are continual changes in: factor prices; technology; product mix; product specifications; social tastes. Failure to understand the impacts of these changing factors can lead to unanticipated impacts on water resources management. Perhaps the most dramatic change in recent years has been the increase in the price of energy.

7) Decisions with respect to water resources management at the level of the individual activity - that is, the water user - are affected by many decisions and factors external to the activity, over which the activity has no control and which are often not related directly to water. Examples include: prices of energy, water, fuel, and prices of other raw material inputs, i.e., chemicals, ores, secondary materials; tax policies; freight rates; tariffs; import, export restrictions. These factors influence decisions on the degree of internal water recirculation and the levels of materials and energy

recovery and by-product production which would take place in the absence of any constraints on residuals discharges to the environment.

8) There are significant short-run variations in: water withdrawals and in the generation and discharge of material and energy reisuduals to water bodies by individual point sources in a river basin; in discharges from nonpoint sources resulting from storms; and in the assimilative capacity of water bodies. Six categories of variations in discharges from point sources are:

    a) Variations during normal operations of an activity, e.g., a manufacturing plant, as a result of changes in product mix, qualities of raw material, operating level;
    b) Start-up/shut-down;
    c) Clean-up;
    d) Upsets during production with no cessation in operations;
    e) Breakdowns such that operations cease; and
    f) Accidental spills.

Variations during "normal" production operations can be subdivided into less than daily and day-to-day variations, less than seasonal production cycle variations reflecting changing product mix, and seasonal variations. Household or residential activities likewise exhibit substantial daily and seasonal variation in water withdrawal, residuals generation, and residuals discharge.

9) The natural systems involved in water resources management - aquatic and terrestrial ecosystems - have assimilative capacities which vary randomly with time: diurnally, daily, seasonally, from year to year. These random variations are superimposed on longer-term climatic trends, shifts, cycles, if any.

If water resources management is to produce the desired outputs, e.g., ambient water quality standards, the variability of both demand and supply must be explicitly considered.

4. Some Specific Considerations

In addition to the "universal" facts of life, in the context of which water resources management in all countries is carried out, there are conditions peculiar to individual countries. Four of these merit mention.

First, depending on the governmental structure of the society, there will be a few or several layers of government with varying responsibilities for parts of water resources management. These layers range from the local level - municipality, township, district - through metropolitan area, county or multicounty, prefecture, soil conservation district, water service area, basin agency, state agencies, inter-state agencies, to the national level. Further, in some countries there are substantial differences among sub-areas of the

country. For example, in the United States some states have integrated natural resources management agencies which include water resources management; some have integrated environmental protection or environmental management agencies which include water resources management; some have separate water resources or water quality boards, commissions, or departments. Each state agency in turn may be organised
differently internally, may have substantially different programmes
and budgetary resources, and substantially different responsibilities.
Similar variations exist at the local level of government.

However water resources management is organised, a critical factor is the relationship of any special water agency - such as a river
basin agency - to the governments of general jurisdiction in the
agency's area. This problem is less critical in countries where there
is a high degree of centralisation in government at the national
level, than where substantial power exists at non-national levels of
government.

Second, in the United States at least, water resources management
is carried out within a complicated milieu of not only multiple agencies, but also of overlapping, mandated water resources planning activities. There are Federal-state river basin commissions covering, in
most cases, lare areas, such as New England, the Great Lakes, the
Pacific Northwest, established under the 1965 Water Resources Planning
Act (Federal). These commissions have responsibility only for planning. Under the Water Pollution Control Act Amendments of 1972
(Public Law 92-500), the states are required to do water quality
management planning on a river basin basis within each state and also
on a metropolitan area basis, where relevant. In addition, various
states have mandated by state legislation the preparation of water
and sewer plans on a county basis, regional (multicounty) water and
sewer plans based on county plans, and state-wide water resources
plans. For example, in the Delaware Basin in the United States, the
State of New Jersey is currently in the process of developing a state
water plan, which will have to be integrated with the Comprehensive
Plan of the Delaware River Basin Commission.

Third, in addition to legislation and regulations directly affecting water resources management, other legislation and regulations
not directed at water per se, impinge indirectly on water resources
management. Examples include legislation and regulations concerning
toxic materials, recycling, used oil.

Fourth, the Swedish approach to environmental problems differs
substantially from the approaches in the other countries. This is
at least partly because there are many water systems in the country
where comparatively high water quality already exists. Therefore
the environmental problems are not of the same degree as in most of
the other countries. Because water quality already is comparatively

18

high, the most efficient way to maintain quality and to improve quality further is considered to be to reduce polluting discharges at
their sources. Therefore, the Swedish system does not start by
stating a desired ambient quality in a water system, as is done in
the other countries, but by stating that each polluter should reduce
discharges as far as possible. In addition, the legislation which
provides for water quality management in Sweden also contains provisions relating to solid wastes, noise, and discharges to the air.

5. Main Characteristics of River Basins Studied

The seven industrialised river basins submitted as national case
studies were clearly chosen because they were interesting examples
of basins that have experienced problems with water quality or quantity. As a result of action plans, water quality in the basins is
being improved and has been at least partially restored to acceptable
conditions. The characteristics of the basins vary significantly not
only physically, in population and in degree of industrialisation,
but in their legal constraints and organisational structures of
management. The Delaware River Basin study concentrates on the
highly industrialised tidal reach of the basin that extends over
200 km inland from the ocean. The area sustains a population of over
7 million - as of 1975 - including Philadelphia and contains one of
the highest concentrations of heavy industry - petroleum refining,
steel, chemicals, paper - in that country. The principal objectives
have been to improve the river quality in this reach mainly for
amenity and environmental purposes. Improvement is being accomplished by massive reductions in the allowable levels of effluent
discharge by municipalities and factories.

The French case study is for the River Oise, a principal tributary of the Seine that joins the main river just downstream from
Paris. It drains an area of nearly 17,000 km^2, has a **population of
1.5 million** - 1975 - and sustains engineering and chemical industries
in the valleys and agricultural activities throughout the area. It
receives the treated municipal effluents from many towns including
that of Reims. The objective has been to retain the quality of water
for amenity, agricultural and public water supply purposes not only
throughout its length but in the lower reaches where water is abstracted for the public supply to Paris. However, most of the data provided cover the whole Seine/Normandy River Basin. The Dommel and Aa
are adjacent tributary basins of the River Meuse in the Netherlands.
They cover 2,750 km^2 of the more elevated land in that country where
there is a population of about 1 million, 43 per cent of which lives
in four large towns. The growth of population and industrialisation
had contributed to a deterioration in river water quality to a point
where it was becoming unsuitable for direct agricultural abstractors.

The objectives have been to restore the quality for these users and for environmental interests; at the moment the needs for public water supply are met from groundwater sources.

The remaining four case studies were for complete river basins, the largest of which was the Trent (United Kingdom) with an area of 10,450 km^2 and a population of 5.9 million -1975-. The majority of the heavy industry and centres of population are in the upper and middle reaches of this system; the Trent itself extending 274 km to the sea. The objective has been to improve the quality of certain stretches and tributaries for amenity and fishery purposes where sewage effluents constitute a large proportion of dry weather flows. Public water supply is provided from groundwater and selected better quality tributaries.

The Yodo Basin (Japan) with an area of 7,300 km^2 and the highest precipitation of 1,500-1,900 mm per annum also has the highest population of nearly 10 million - 1975 - and supplies water for over 14 million. The largest concentration of population and industry is at Osaka at the lower end of the Basin but it also supplies water and accepts effluents from Kyoto in the middle reaches. Flows are regulated by storage in the large Lake Biwa and reservoirs in the upper reaches.

The Swedish case study is of the Kävlingean Basin. The Kävlingean River is a 95 km long river that stretches inland from the coast in southwest Sweden in a basin covering 1,200 km^2. It has storage lakes in the upper reaches from which water is exported from the basin to provide a public supply for Malmö. Within the basin the main centres of demand for industry and public water supply are in the middle to lower reaches. It receives municipal effluents and those from a variety of agricultural industries (sugar beet processing, slaughter houses, tanneries etc.).

The Parramatta Basin (Australia) of 123 km^2 is the smallest basin studied. It lies within part of metropolitan Sydney. The -1975- resident population is 0.6 million and urban and industrial land use comprise 55 per cent of the total. After a 40 per cent expansion of population in 20 years and large extension of chemical and engineering industries in the lower reaches, severe pollution was experienced. However, the river is now virtually unpolluted in dry weather conditions.

Figures 1-2 through 1-8 show the Trent (England), Parramatta (Australia), Yodo (Japan), Dommel/Aa (the Netherlands), Delaware (United States), Kävlingean (Sweden), and Seine/Normandy (France) River Basins, respectively. Selected characteristics of the basins are presented in Table 1-1.

Table 1-1

SELECTED CHARACTERISTICS OF RIVER BASINS STUDIED

	Trent (U.K.)[a]	Parramatta (Australia)	Yodo (Japan)	Kävlingean (Sweden)
Basin area, km^2	10,450	123	7,300	1,217
River length, km	274	20	153	95
Tidal length, km	97	18	9.4	0
Range in elevation, m	200-sea level	200-sea level	85-sea level	160-sea level
Mean annual precipitation, mm	734	–	1745	600 ± 10
Range in precipitation, mm	570-1500	840-1220	1560-1920	392-972
Mean river flow, m^3/sec	84^b	nil (in dry weather)	215^d	11^f
Population, 1975, 10^6	5.9	$0.64/2.8^c$	$9.7/14.3^e$	0.053^g
Proportion in urban area	about 50%	100%	26%	about 50%
Major activities	Mining, agriculture, industry	Primarily residential; urban, some industrial	Industry, housing, agriculture	Primarily agriculture; some industry, primarily food processing
Surface water regulation by	Reservoirs	Lake and reservoirs	Lake Biwa and reservoirs	Lake Vombsjön
Major conurbations in or served by water from basin	Birmingham, Nottingham, Leicester, Stoke	Sydney	Kyoto, Osaka	Malmo, Lund

	Dommel/Aa (Netherlands)	Seine/Normandie (France)	Delaware (U.S.)
Basin area, km^2	$2700/2300^h$	96,645	34,000
River length, km	78/65	776	426
Tidal length, km	0	0	185
Range in elevation, m	35-5	367-23	914-sea level
Mean annual precipitation, mm	775	–	1130
Range in precipitation, mm	600-900	600-1150	1020-1520
Mean river flow, m^3/sec	19	110	322
Population, 1975, 10^6	1.2^i	1.5	7
Proportion in urban area, %	43%	?	75-80%
Major activities	Primarily agriculture, one major industrial conurbation	Industry, agriculture, food processing	Heavily industrialised in estuary area; recreation in upper basin; mining
Surface water regulation by	weir and small reservoir	Reservoirs	Reservoirs
Major conurbations in or served by water from basin	Eindhoven	Paris	New York City, Philadelphia

a) U.K. in this report refers only to England and Wales.

b) River Trent at Nottingham, 11 years of record.

c) 0.64 in catchments of Parramatta and Lane Cove; 2.8 in Sydney metropolitan area.

d) Yodo River at Hirakata; "ordinary" (approximately median) flow.

e) 9.7 in Yodo river basin; 14.3 in area supplied by water from Yodo.

f) Flow to the estuary.

g) Population as of 1965.

h) 2,700 km^2 total; 2,300 in the Netherlands.

i) No date specified.

Note: No period of record is cited in any of the data submitted for either precipitation or river flow.

Figure 1.2

RIVER TRENT BASIN

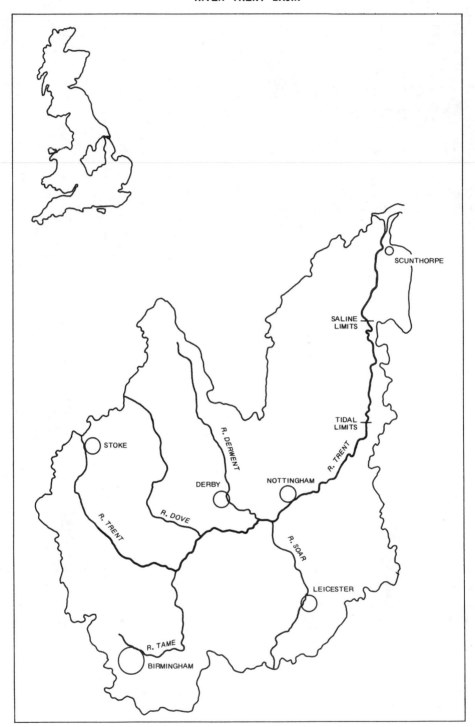

Figure 1.3

STATE POLLUTION CONTROL COMMISSION

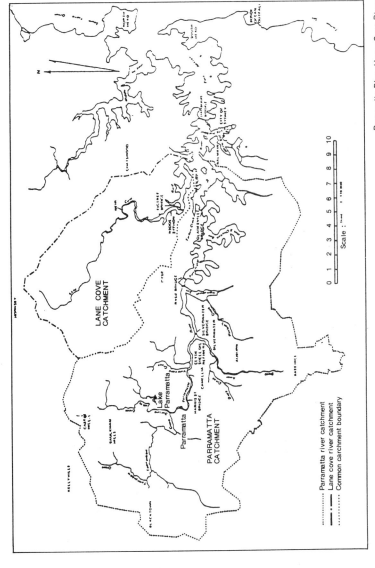

Parramatta River/ Lane Cove River
– Catchments

Map 2

23

Figure 1.4

**MAIN WATER RESOURCES DEVELOPMENT FACILITIES
IN THE YODO RIVER BASIN**

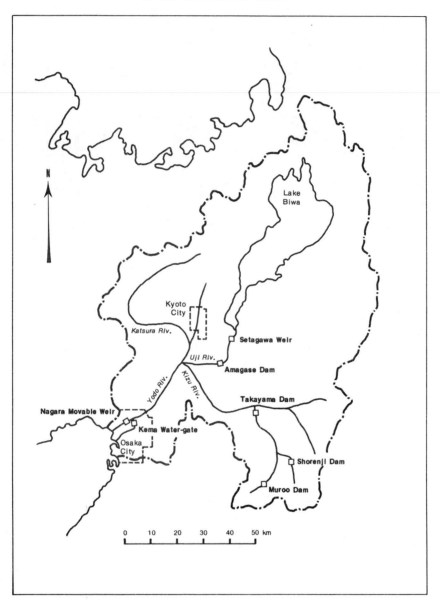

Figure 1.5

CATCHMENT OF RIVERS DOMMEL AND AA

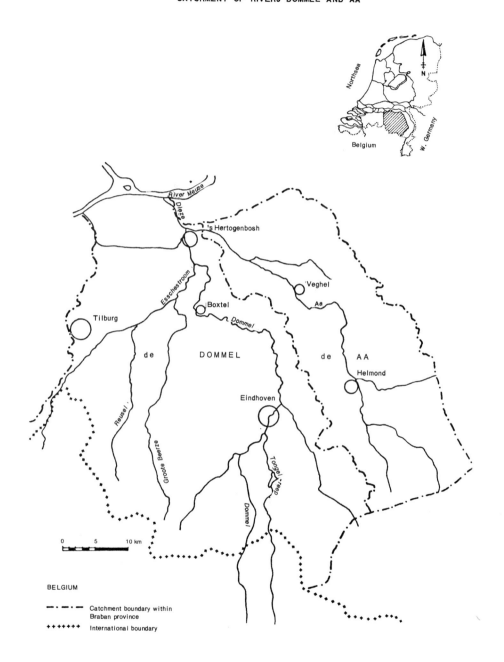

Figure 1.6

DELAWARE RIVER BASIN AND SUBBASINS*

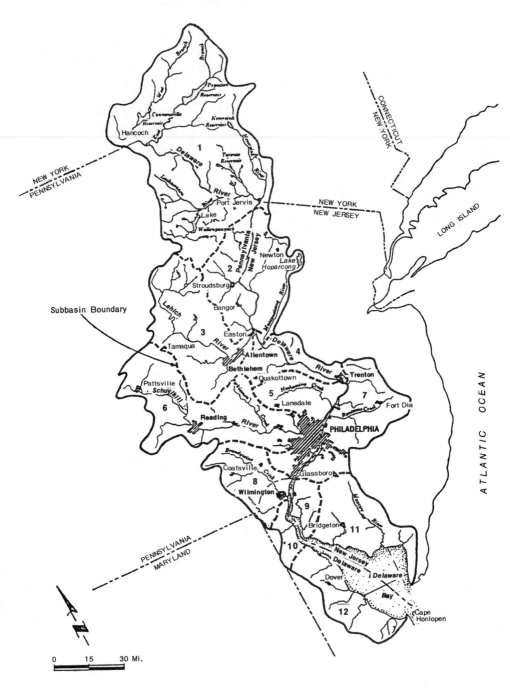

* Reference 10

Figure 1.7

KÄVLINGEAN RIVER BASIN

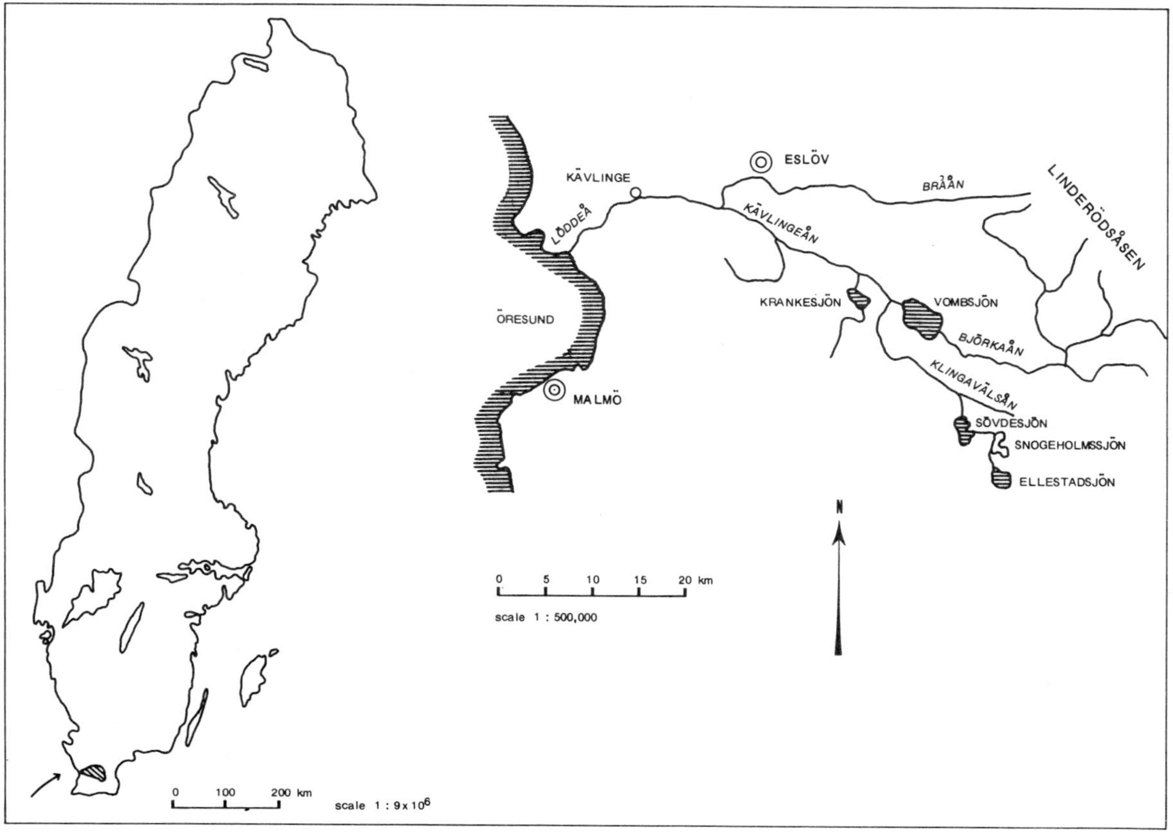

LINDERÖDSÅSEN

BRÅÅN

VOMBSJÖN

BJÖRKAÅN

KLINGAVÄLSÅN

SÖVDESJÖN

SNOGEHOLMSSJÖN

ELLESTADSJÖN

ESLÖV

KÄVLINGEÅN

KRANKESJÖN

N

KÄVLINGE

LÖDDEÅ

ÖRESUND

MALMÖ

scale 1 : 500,000

0   5   10   15   20 km

0   100   200 km

scale 1 : 9 x 10⁶

Figure 1.8

L'OISE ET L'AISNE DANS LE BASSIN SEINE-NORMANDIE

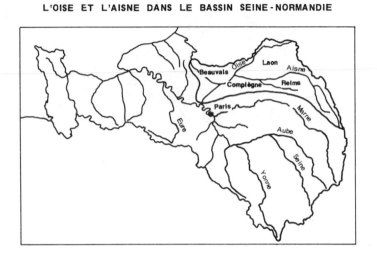

PHYSICAL CHARACTERISTICS OF WATERSHED OF RIVER OISE

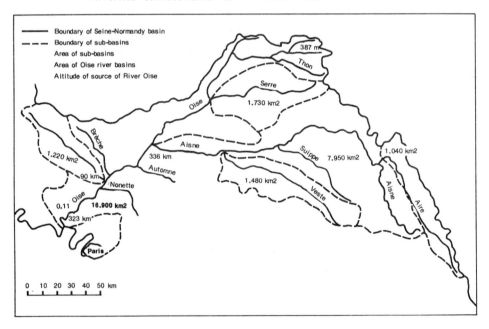

Chapter II

ESTABLISHMENT OF AMBIENT WATER QUALITY STANDARDS

Ambient water quality standards may be established for all types of water bodies, including ground waters, rivers, lakes, estuaries, and coastal waters. Three levels of ambient water quality standards can be identified, in terms of increasing degrees of specificity: (1) no ambient water quality standards; (2) general water quality standards using terms such as "protected", "controlled", "restricted", or terms relating to use of the water body, such as for drinking water, bathing, agriculture; and (3) quantitative limits for a number of specific water quality indicators, without or with linkage of the quantitative limits to specific water uses.

Sweden has not established ambient water quality standards, except as standards are implied in such language as, "disturbances must be prevented" and nuisances should be avoided or rectified. The New South Wales (Australia) Clean Waters Act (enacted 1972) represents the use of general water quality standards. This Act provides for the following classifications of waters:

Class S, Specially protected waters;
Class P, Protected waters;
Class C, Controlled waters;
Class R, Restricted waters;
Class O, Ocean outfall waters; and
Class U, Underground waters.

The third degree of specificity, that is, where water quality standards are expressed in terms of quantitative limits for a number of water quality indicators, is exemplified by the Japanese system; the United States system, and the recently adopted United Kingdom system. In Japan, ambient water quality standards are divided into: (1) those related to protection of human health; and (2) those related to conservation of the living environment. The former standards apply uniformly to all Japanese surface water bodies, and are listed in Table II-1.

Table II-1

JAPANESE AMBIENT WATER QUALITY STANDARDS FOR
PROTECTION OF HUMAN HEALTH, AS OF FEBRUARY 1975

Water Quality Indicator	Standard(a)
Cadmium	0.01 ppm or less
Cyanide	Not detectable(b)
Organic phosphorus(c)	Not detectable
Lead	0.1 ppm or less
Chromium (hexavalent)	0.05 ppm or less
Arsenic	0.05 ppm or less
Total mercury(d)	0.0005 ppm or less
Alkyl mercury	Not detectable
PCB	Not detectable

a) Maximum values. With regard to total mercury, the standard
   is based on the yearly average value.
b) "Not detectable" means that the substance is below the level
   detectable by the specified method of measurement.
c) Organic phosphorus includes parathion, methyl parathon,
   methyl demeton, and E.P.N.
d) The standard for total mercury is 0.001 ppm or less in case
   it is obvious that pollution in rivers is caused by natural
   factors.

The United States approach is exemplified in Table II-2, which shows
ambient water quality standards for Zone 2 of the Delaware River Basin.

In the United Kingdom, ambient water quality standards previously were expressed in terms of the objectives, "to maintain or restore
the wholesomeness of the rivers", as indicated by a quality which
would enable reasonable fisheries to exist, and - in heavily urbanised
and industrial areas - to avoid nuisance or obvious visual pollution.
However, quantitative standards, shown in Table II-3, have recently
been adopted. These standards correspond to those adopted by the
EEC.

Table II-2

AMBIENT WATER QUALITY STANDARDS FOR ZONE 2, DELAWARE RIVER BASIN

3.30.1 <u>Application</u> (Resolution No. 67-7). This Article shall apply to the Delaware River Estuary and Bay, including the tidal portions of the tributaries thereof.

3.30.2 <u>Zone 2</u>

A. <u>Description</u> (Resolution No. 67-7). Zone 2 is that part of the Delaware River extending from the head of tide-water at Trenton, New Jersey, R.M. (River Mile) 133.4 (Trenton-Morrisville Toll Bridge) to R.M. 108.4 below the mouth of Pennypack Creek, including the tidal portions of the tributaries thereof.

B. <u>Water uses to be protected</u> (Resolution No. 74-1). The quality of Zone 2 waters shall be maintained in a safe and satisfactory condition for the following uses:

1. a) public water supplies after reasonable treatment,
   b) industrial water supplies after reasonable treatment,
   c) agricultural water supplies;

2. a) maintenance and propagation of resident fish and other aquatic life,
   b) passage of anadromous fish,
   c) wildlife;

3. a) recreation from R.M. 133.4 to R.M. 117.81,
   b) recreation - secondary contact from R.M. 177.81 to R.M. 108.4;

4. navigation.

C. <u>Stream quality objectives</u>

1. Dissolved oxygen (Resolution No. 74-1)

   a) 24-hour average concentration shall not be less than 5.0 mg/l.
   b) During the periods from 1st April to 15th June, and 16th September to 31st December, the dissolved oxygen shall not have a seasonal average less than 6.5 mg/l.

2. Temperature (Resolution No. 74-1). Shall not exceed:

   a) 5°F (2.8°C) above the average 24-hour temperature gradient displayed during the 1961-66 period, or
   b) a maximum of 86°F (30.0°C), whichever is less.

3. <u>pH</u> (Resolution No. 67-7). Between 6.5 and 8.5.

4. <u>Phenols</u> (Resolution No. 74-1). Maximum 0.005 mg/l, unless exceeded due to natural conditions.

5. <u>Threshold odour number</u> (Resolution No. 67-7). Not to exceed 24 at 60°C.

6. <u>Synthetic detergents</u> (M.B.A.S.) (Resolution No. 74-1). Maximum 30-day average 0.5 mg/l.

7. <u>Radioactivity</u> (Resolution No. 67-7)

   a) alpha emitters - maximum 3 pc/l (picocuries per litre);
   b) beta emitters - maximum 1,000 pc/l.

8. <u>Fecal coliform</u> (Resolution No. 74-1). Maximum geometric average

   a) 200 per 100 millilitres above R.M. 117-81;
   b) 770 per 100 millilitres below R.M. 117.81.

      Samples shall be taken at such frequency and location as to permit valid interpretation.

9. <u>Total dissolved solids</u> (Resolution No. 74-1). Not to exceed:

   a) 133 per cent of background, or
   b) 500 mg/l, whichever is less.

10. <u>Turbidity</u> (Resolution No. 74-1). Unless exceeded due to natural conditions:

    a) maximum 30-day average 40 units;
    b) maximum 150 units;
    c) except above R.M. 117.81 during the period 30th May to 15th September when the turbidity shall not exceed 30 units.

11. <u>Alkalinity</u> (Resolution No. 67-7). Between 20 and 100 mg/l.

12. <u>Chlorides</u> (Resolution No. 74-1). Maximum 15-day average 50 mg/l.

13. <u>Hardness</u> (Resolution No. 74-1). Maximum 30-day average 95 mg/l.

Table II-3

- AMBIENT WATER STANDARDS -
TRENT RIVER BASIN

River Class	Quality criteria	Remarks	Current potential uses
	Class limiting criteria (95 percentile)		
1A	(i) Dissolved oxygen saturation greater than 80 per cent. (ii) Biochemical oxygen demand not greater than 3 mg/l. (iii) Ammonia not greater than 0.4 mg/l. (iv) Where the water is abstracted for drinking water, it complies with requirements for A2** water. (v) Non-toxic to fish in EIFAC terms (or best estimates if EIFAC figures not available).	(i) Average BOD probably not greater than 1.5 mg/l. (ii) Visible evidence of pollution should be absent.	(i) Water of high quality supply for potable supply abstractions and for all other abstractions. (ii) Game or other high class fisheries. (iii) High amenity value.
1B	(i) DO greater than 60 per cent saturation. (ii) BOD not greater than 5 mg/l. (iii) Ammonia not greater than 0.9 mg/l. (iv) Where water is abstracted for drinking water, it complies with the requirements for A2** water. (v) Non-toxic to fish in EIFAC terms (or best estimates if EIFAC figures not available).	(i) Average BOD probably not greater than 2 mg/l. (ii) Average ammonia probably not greater than 0.5 mg/l. (iii) Visible evidence of pollution should be absent. (iv) Waters of high quality which cannot be placed in Class 1A because of high proportion of high quality effluent present or because of the effect of physical factors such as canalisation low gradient or eutrophication. (v) Class 1A and Class 1B together are essentially the Class 1 of the River Pollution Survey.	Water of less high quality than Class 1A but usable for substantially the same purposes.
2	(i) DO greater than 40 per cent saturation. (ii) BOD not greater than 9 mg/l. (iii) Where water is abstracted for drinking water, it complies with the requirements for A3** water. (iv) Non-toxic to fish in EIFAC terms (or best estimates if EIFAC figures not available).	(i) Average BOD probably not greater than 5mg/l. (ii) Similar to Class 2 of RPS. (iii) Water not showing physical signs of pollution other than humic colouration and a little foaming below weirs.	(i) Waters suitable for potable supply after advanced treatment. (ii) Supporting reasonably good coarse fisheries. (iii) Moderate amenity value

River Class	Quality criteria — Class limiting criteria (95 percentile)	Remarks	Current potential uses
3	(i) DO greater than 10 per cent saturation. (ii) Not likely to be anaerobic. (iii) BOD not greater than 17 mg/l*.	Similar to Class 3 of RPS.	Waters which are polluted to an extent that fish are absent or only sporadically present. May be used for low grade industrial abstraction purposes. Considerable potential for further use if cleaned up.
4	Waters which are inferior to Class 3 in terms of dissolved oxygen and likely to be anaerobic at times.	Similar to Class 4 of RPS.	Waters which are grossly polluted and are likely to cause nuisance.
X	DO greater than 10 per cent saturation.		Insignificant watercourses and ditches not usable, where objective is simply to prevent nuisance developing.

Note:

a) Under extreme weather conditions (e.g. flood, drought, freeze-up), or when dominated by plant growth, or by aquatic plant decay, rivers usually in Classes 1, 2 and 3 may have BODs and dissolved oxygen levels, or ammonia content outside the stated levels for those Classes. When this occurs the cause should be stated along with analytical results.

b) The BOD determinations refer to 5 day carbonaceous BOD (ATU). Ammonia figures are expressed as NH_4.

c) In most instances the chemical classification given above will be suitable. However, the basis of the classification is restricted to a finite number of chemical determinants and there may be a few cases where the presence of a chemical substance other than those used in the classification markedly reduces the quality of the water. In such cases, the quality classification of the water should be downgraded on the basis of the biota actually present, and the reasons stated.

d) EIFAC (European Inland Fisheries Advisory Commission) limits should be expressed as 95 per cent percentile limits.

* This may not apply if there is a high degree of re-aeration.

** EEC category A2 and A3 requirements are those specified in the EEC Council Directive of 16th June, 1975 concerning the Quality of Surface Water intended for Abstraction of Drinking Water in the Member States.

28th January, 1977.

Seven other points with respect to the establishment of ambient water quality standards can be made, based on the seven case studies.

1. Typically, different standards are established for different sections of a river or an estuary, at least where such water bodies are of substantial length, have varying uses in different sections, and have varying assimilative capacities in different sections. For example, the water quality class for the main stem of the Yodo River from its confluence with the Uji River to just downstream from Nayara movable weir is class B, the remainder of the main stem to Osaka Bay is class D. The Uji River, a major tributary of the Yodo, is class A for about two-thirds of its length, class B for the remainder to its confluence with the Yodo. In the Delaware Basin five water quality zones are delineated between the head of the estuary and the mouth of Delaware Bay at the Atlantic Ocean. The first four zones comprise the Delaware estuary, the fifth zone is the Delaware Bay. The differences in water quality standards are based on different water use patterns in the different sections of the water body.

2. Standards may be changed as new or additional information is obtained about specific pollutants. Thus, the standards promulgated in Japan for protection of human health in 1971 were modified with respect to concentrations of total mercury and alkyl mercury in September 1974 and a PCB standard was added in February 1975.

3. The stochastic nature of streamflow has not always been explicitly considered in the establishment of standards. Flow conditions are rarely specified for which the ambient standards are to be achieved. In Japan, the standards for the protection of human health are to be met regardless of the quantity of flow, whereas the standards for conservation of the living environment are to be met under low flow conditions, which are defined as the flow equalled or exceeded 75 per cent of the time. In some cases, the ten-year, seven-day low flow is used as the base for the water quality standards. Such an approach assumes that if the standards can be achieved under the flow conditions with that recurrence interval, they can be achieved a high proportion of the time.

4. Ambient water quality standards can be varied by season, to reflect differences in water uses. For example, for the Delaware estuary, the dissolved oxygen standard is higher during shad migration seasons in the spring (1st April - 15th June) and fall (16th September - 31st December) than during the remainder of the year.

5. Although not made explicit, the quantitative standards established for various water quality indicators are based on various studies relating water quality to particular uses, such as for fisheries, agriculture, drinking water. In the United States, several lengthy studies of water quality criteria have been done in the last twenty-five years.

6. Ambient water quality standards are established by different procedures and by different governmental agencies, or mixes of agencies, in the different countries. In Japan, the authority for establishing standards is delegated to the prefecture, except for water bodies involving more than one prefecture. The prefecture determines the classification of various water bodies or sections thereof in relation to uses of the water bodies to which the standards for the living environment then apply. (As noted previously, the standards for protection of human health, Table II-1, apply to all water bodies.) In Australia, the state government classifies water bodies. In France, the national government develops a table relating water uses to specific levels of various water quality indicators. The river basin agencies then decide into which class to place each river reach. In the Netherlands, the river basin waterboards (Waterschappen) establish the standards for non-national waters, the national government for national waters.

7. Relatively few ambient water quality standards have been developed this far with respect to toxic materials.

In the United States, each state must establish ambient water quality standards, which then must be approved by the federal government. The procedure was somewhat different in the Delaware Basin, because the Delaware River Basin Commission was in existence before the 1965 legislation requiring the state-federal standard-setting procedure was passed. In the Delaware Basin the procedure involved a detailed study of the estuary, using a water quality model. Five levels of quality were investigated - each involving a set of water quality indicators - with the levels representing increasingly stringent water quality targets. The costs to achieve each set were estimated, and the benefits associated with each set - primarily water-based recreation and fish production/survival - were estimated. Public hearings were held, further analyses with the model were made, and then the Commission made its decision on the standards to be achieved. It should be noted, however, that prior to the 1965 federal legislation mandating the establishment of ambient water quality standards by each state, the states had the authority and responsibility to establish standards. Many of them had done so, either on an intra-state basis or on an interstate basis through an interstate agency such as the Ohio River Valley Sanitation Commission.

Table II-4 summarises information available with respect to the establishment of ambient water quality standards in the river basins investigated in the study.

The following generalisation appears valid, based on the data presented: the degree of quantification and the number of water quality indicators used in establishing ambient water quality standards are a function of the complexity of the water quality management problem in the given basin. Complexity is a function of the magnitudes and diversity of activities in a basin, in relation to the available assimilative capacity. The scarcer the capacity in relation to demand on the water resource and the wider the diversity of activities generating and discharging more types of residuals, the greater the tendency toward quantification of ambient water quality standards and the greater the tendency toward including more water quality indicators. Both increasing quantification and increasing number of indicators are also probably a function of increasing knowledge about the impacts of various materials on the environment and on human beings.

Table II-4

DATA RELATING TO ESTABLISHMENT OF AMBIENT WATER
QUALITY STANDARDS IN SEVEN RIVER BASINS

River Basin	Type of ambient water quality standards	Standards varied by season	Flow conditions specified for standards	Level of government establishing standards
Trent (U.K.)	Quantitative limits	No	No	River basin agency
Parramatta (Australia)	General categories	No	No	State government
Yodo (Japan)	Quantitative limits	No	Yes	National and Prefectural governments
Kävlingean (Sweden)	No specific standards	–	–	–
Dommel/Aa (the Netherlands)	Quantitative limits	No	No	Waterboards, national government
Seine/Normandie (France)	Quantitative limits	No	Yes	National government, river basin agencies
Delaware (U.S.)	Quantitative limits	Yes	Implicit in analysis	River basin commission(a)

a) Delaware River Basin Commission established the ambient water quality standards for the Delaware Basin. However, as noted in the text, this was an exception. The normal procedure is for each state to establish the standards, which standards must be approved by the federal government.

37

Chapter III

ESTABLISHMENT OF EMISSION (DISCHARGE) CONTROLS

INTRODUCTION

Definitions

To provide a common basis for the subsequent discussion, some definitions are necessary. Figure III-1 provides a pictorial representation of the basic options involved in water abstractions and wastewater discharges.

Abstraction = intake = withdrawal: the quantity of water taken in at the intake of the water system of an activity, which intake may be the end of a pipe in a surface water body, a well tapping a ground water aquifer, or the beginning of the pipe connection from a communal water distribution system to the individual activity.

Emission = discharge = effluent: the quantity of water and contained materials and heat passing beyond the boundary of an activity - point or non-point - and entering a surface or ground water body or a communal sewer system.

Withdrawal standard (abstraction condition): a condition imposed on the quantity, time pattern, and/or location of a withdrawal.

Discharge standard: a condition imposed on the quantity, quality, time pattern, and/or location of a discharge (see Table III-1).

License or permit: an authorisation given by a governmental body to withdraw water or discharge wastewater under specified conditions, e.g., quantity, time pattern, location of withdrawal or discharge, special limitations under drought conditions, requirements for self-measuring/monitoring; analogous to a business permit, e.g., a condition of doing business.

Fee: the amount of money which must be paid to obtain a permit or a license, e.g., a license fee; may be a one-time fee or an annual fee. It is payment for the authorisation to withdraw or to discharge, and must be paid regardless of whether or not a withdrawal or discharge is made.

38

Figure 3-1

CONFIGURATIONS OF ABSTRACTIONS AND DISCHARGES
CONFIGURATION DES PRELEVEMENTS ET DES REJETS

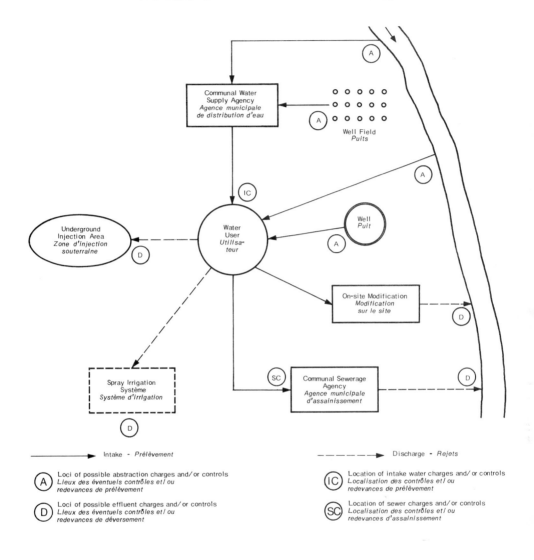

Abstraction (withdrawal) charge: amount of money paid for withdrawing water from a surface or ground water body, based either on each volumetric unit of water withdrawn or on each unit of water flow (flow rate, e.g., litres per second) withdrawn.

User charge: amount of money paid for a service rendered, e.g., treating intake water to potable standards, developing a reservoir and piping system to convey water to individual users, treating wastewater.

In the United Kingdom the term trade effluent charge is used to refer to charges paid by industrialists for the discharge of their industrial waste waters to the municipal sewerage system for subsequent treatment at the sewage treatment works owned and operated by the Regional Water Authorities'.

Effluent charge: conceptually it is a payment for use of the assimilative capacity of the environment, and is imposed on each unit of residual (material and energy) discharged to a surface or ground water body.

Operationally an effluent charge is conceived of as an economic incentive to induce reduction in discharge. However, only if the charge is high enough will it act as an incentive to reduce discharges. If the charge is less than the marginal cost of reducing discharge for most discharges, there will be little incentive effect and the charge simply becomes a means of raising revenue. (The same is true for user charges. If such charges are high enough, they will be incentives for discharges to reduce their discharges.)

Pollution charge: as used herein, includes both user charges and effluent charges; is applied to each unit of pollutant.

Tax: a payment exacted by a governmental body in order to raise revenue, e.g., personal and corporate income tax, VAT, sales tax, real estate tax.

Types of Standards/Charges Systems to Induce Reductions in Discharges

The objective of any operational system of effluent standards, effluent charges, and combinations of standards and charges is to induce reductions in discharges such that the ambient standards will be met. What per cent of time the ambient standards will be met is a function of the extent to which the effluent standards/effluent charges system takes into consideration the variability of residuals generation and the variability of the natural assimilative capacities of water bodies.

Five types of systems appear to exist at present, or to have been seriously considered.

1) effluent standards only, in terms of total quantity discharged per day, concentration of discharge, both;
2) effluent standards with effluent charges on all discharges above an upper limit;
3) effluent standards with effluent charges on all discharges, the rationale being that the charges will: a) hasten the achievement of the effluent standards; b) provide a continuing incentive to reduce discharges below the standard; and c) raise revenues for water quality management investments and activities;

4) effluent charges only; and

5) effluent charges with an upper limit on the total quantity of discharge permitted per day.

Conceptually, all systems could be varied in relation to flow conditions, as is the case with some abstraction charges. All systems are applied to only a few of the many materials which are, or might be, discharged to water bodies.

A. EMISSION (DISCHARGE) STANDARDS

Conceptually, discharge (emission, effluent) standards – as well as effluent charges – for direct discharges into surface or ground water bodies should be developed and imposed in relation to the desired ambient water quality standards to be achieved, as depicted in Figure III-2. This requires one or more water quality models which can transform the time and spatial pattern of residuals discharges into the resulting time and spatial pattern of ambient water quality. However, where rough or simple water quality models, e.g., volumetric, are adequate to indicate that ambient water quality standards can readily be met if all dischargers adopt reasonable practices, then analysis using more complex water quality models is not necessary. In addition, verified water quality models do not exist for all types of discharges. At present, the behaviour of degradable organic materials, suspended solids, total dissolved solids ("salinity"), and nutrients (N & P) have been most successfully modelled.

It should be noted that the Swedish approach to setting discharge standards does not explicitly consider ambient water quality standards. Rather, it is assumed that if dischargers meet the technology based discharge standards, acceptable ambient water quality will result.

Standards imposed on the discharge of residuals – material and energy – can be expressed in various ways, both with respect to discharges directly to surface and ground water bodies and with respect to discharges to communal (municipal, metropolitan area, sanitation district) facilities. Standards can be applied to both point and non-point sources.

To preclude misunderstanding, it is important to distinguish between direct discharge standards – those which are related directly to the quantity and/or quality of the discharge – and indirect discharge standards. Indirect standards are implicit only, because they do not relate directly to the quantity and/or quality of the discharge but rather are expressed in terms of required production processes, required residuals modification processes, limits on types and/or quantities of inputs, specifications of final product outputs,

41

Figure 3-2

PROCEDURE FOR DEVELOPING DISCHARGE STANDARDS BASED ON AMBIENT WATER QUALITY STANDARDS
PROCEDURE DE DETERMINATION DE NORMES DE DEVERSEMENT BASEES SUR DES NORMES DE QUALITE

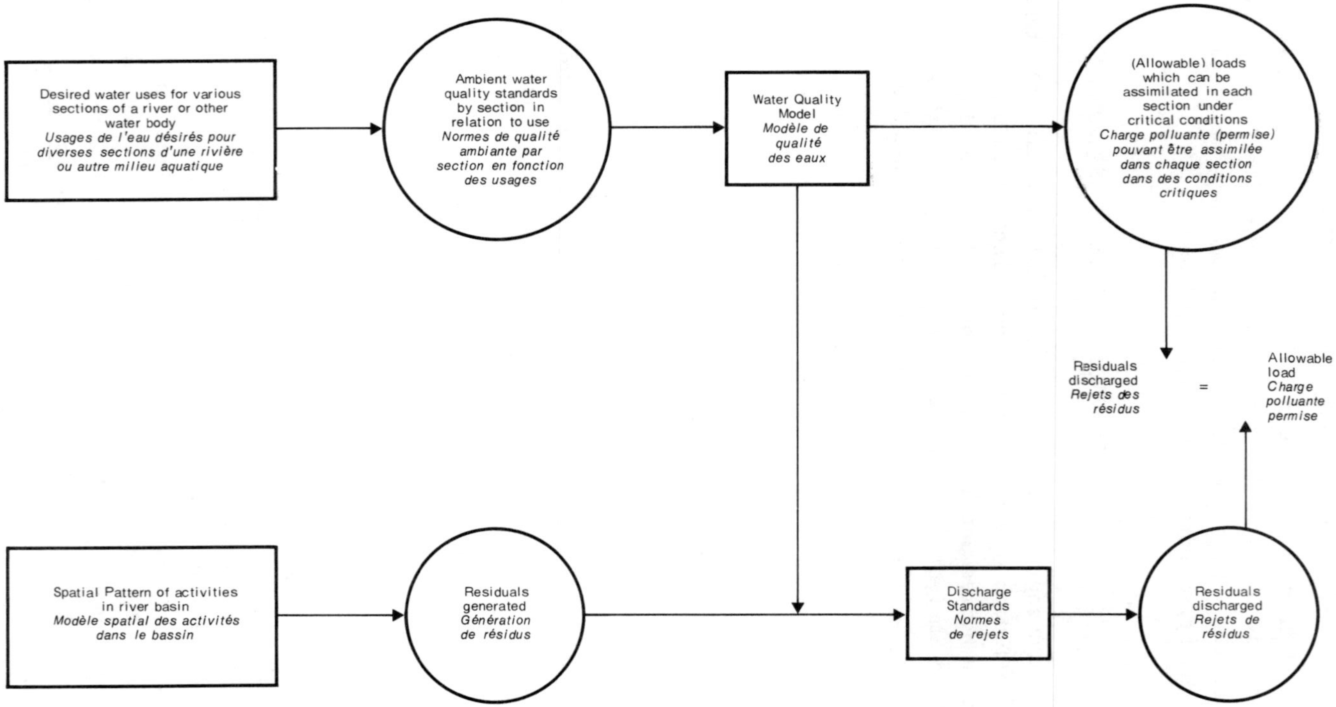

Desired water uses for various sections of a river or other water body
Usages de l'eau désirés pour diverses sections d'une rivière ou autre milieu aquatique

Ambient water quality standards by section in relation to use
Normes de qualité ambiante par section en fonction des usages

Water Quality Model
Modèle de qualité des eaux

(Allowable) loads which can be assimilated in each section under critical conditions
Charge polluante (permise) pouvant être assimilée dans chaque section dans des conditions critiques

Residuals discharged
Rejets des résidus

=

Allowable load
Charge polluante permise

Residuals discharged
Rejets de résidus

Discharge Standards
Normes de rejets

Residuals generated
Génération de résidus

Spatial Pattern of activities in river basin
Modèle spatial des activités dans le bassin

42

such as prohibiting or limiting the phosphate content in detergents.
The application of the physical measures specified by these indirect
standards is _assumed_ to result in an acceptable quality of discharge.
Table III-1 lists examples of both direct and indirect discharge
standards.

The discharge standards listed in Table III-1 can be applied
singly or in various combinations, and can be applied differently in
different times of the year to reflect differences in assimilative
capacity and/or water uses. The first three types of direct standards
listed can be applied to one or several residuals discharged from
an activity and can be expressed in terms of a mean value, a frequency distribution, or a mean with a maximum permitted. For example, the mean discharge permitted may be X kilogrammes per ton,
thirty-day mean, with a maximum of 2X kilogrammes per ton one day
in thirty.

Both indirect and direct discharge standards may be applied
simultaneously, e.g., a permit can specify that an activated sludge
plant must be installed and the concentrations of BOD_5 and total
suspended solids in the discharge can be no more than 30 mg/l. A
discharge standard in terms of kilogrammes per ton of product or per
unit of raw material processed is coupled with a level of total product output or total raw material processed per day to yield an
allowable total kilogrammes of discharge per day.

Both direct and indirect discharge standards can be, and have
been, applied to non-point, as well as to point sources. In some
agricultural areas in the United States, soil loss limits in terms
of tons/acre are imposed. Alternatively or simultaneously, best
management practices are specified for each combination of crop
type-land class on a farm, e.g., type of plowing, degree of tillage,
extent and type of terrace construction. Typical indirect discharge
standards applied to construction sites in the United States include
an upper limit, e.g., 10 per cent on the amount of soil without vege-
tative cover at any time, and the required placing of bales of hay
around the perimeter of the site.

In all river basins studied, except the Yodo Basin in Japan,
point sources must obtain permits or licences to discharge. In the
Yodo Basin, a discharger must report in detail about specified facilities and effluent discharged therefrom, but he does not have to
obtain a permit.

There may be a limit on the size of the operation or the size
of the discharge, below which a permit is not required. In some
cases a fee is charged for the permit. The size of the fee may depend on the size of the operation or the size of the discharge or
both. The permit specifies the standards, the self-monitoring

Table III-1

Direct and Indirect Discharge Standards

DIRECT DISCHARGE STANDARDS(a)

Discharge per unit of product or per unit of raw material processed should be no more than a specified amount, e.g., X kilogrammes of suspended solids per ton of steel produced, Y kilogrammes of BOD_5 per barrel of crude petroleum processed.

Total quantity of discharge per unit of time should be no more than a specified amount, e.g., Z kilogrammes of COD per day.

Concentrations of discharge should be no more than a specified level, e.g., 30 mg/l of total suspended solids.

Degree of variation in quantity of discharge is limited, e.g., maximum instantaneous discharge can be no more than 10 per cent larger than the daily mean.

Discharge is permitted only at certain times of day, week, season.

Discharge is permitted only in certain locations (e.g., certain river reaches, sections of estuary).

INDIRECT DISCHARGE STANDARDS

Best practical, best available technology of production must be used, e.g., oxygen bleaching in pulp mill, contour plowing and minimum tillage in agriculture, skyline logging in timber harvesting (specification of production process)(b).

Best practical, best available residuals modification technology must be used, e.g., activated sludge, cyanide recovery (specification of treatment process)(b).

Limitation on materials in product, e.g., phosphate in detergent must be no more than 5 per cent by weight (specification of product characteristics)(c).

Limitation on material inputs, e.g., no more than 50 kilogrammes of nitrogen can be applied per acre.

---

a) Performance standards.
b) Process standards.
c) Product standards.

requirements if any, and the length of time the permit applies before renewal is required. (Elaboration with respect to licence fees
is found in paragraph B.)

Actual permits are usually specified on a case-by-case basis,
e.g., for each discharger. However there may be, as in the United
States and France, extensive "guidelines" for each industrial or
activity category, which comprise the basis for individual permits.
The concept under the United States Water Pollution Control Act
Amendments of 1972 was that all plants in the same subcategory should
have the same discharge standards, except where the assimilative
capacity of the stream was insufficient such that greater reduction
in discharge would be required to meet ambient water quality
standards.

Factors which may be considered in establishing discharge standards include:

Assimilative capacity of the water body, and its variation by
time of year;
Existing ambient water quality standards;
Uses of the water body, and associated benefits;
Available production process and residuals modification tech-
nology, both domestic and international;
Variability in residuals generation;
Whether or not toxic residuals are generated;
Costs to discharger of reducing discharges, in relation to
present (and/or future) profitability of the enterprise;
Employment effects in region if costs of reducing discharges
were to "sink" the enterprise;
State of the national economy; and
Effect on international competitive position.

In the Seine/Normandie river basin, the goal - not yet realised -
is to establish discharge standards on the basis of equal marginal
costs of discharge reduction.

A permit may contain standards relating to only one or two residuals, or to as many as fifteen or twenty. The permitted discharge
of one or more of these may be determined by use of a water quality
model and some load allocation principle, as was done in the Delaware
Basin (United States).

A permit is usually issued for a limited period of time. Any
significant change in level of output, or modification of production
process, or change in raw materials normally requires the discharger
to obtain a revised permit.

Available information with respect to discharge standards in
the river basins investigated in the study is summarised in
tables III-2 and III-3. The former presents characteristics of discharge standards and the latter presents factors considered in establishing discharge standards.

Table III-2

Characteristics of Discharge Standards in Seven River Basins

Characteristics	Trent (U.K.)	River Basin		Kavlingean (Sweden)
		Parramatta (Australia)	Yodo (Japan)	
Type of discharge standard	Direct	Direct	Direct	Indirect & Direct
Permit or license required to discharge	Yes	Yes	No(a)	Yes(b)
Duration of permit,(c) years until renewal required	Indefinite	1	–	Indefinite
Fee imposed for permit	No	Yes, based on volume per day	–	No
Standards imposed on non-point sources	No	?	No	No
Standards imposed on discharges to underground strata	Yes	Yes	(e)	No
Form of discharge(d) standards	Concentration & quantity	Concentration & quantity	Concentration	Technical requirements, concentration, quantity

Characteristics	Dommel/Aa (Netherlands)	River Basin Seine/Normandie (France)	Delaware (U.S.)
Type of discharge standard	Direct	Direct	Direct
Permit of license required to discharge	Yes	Yes	Yes
Duration of permit, years until renewal required	Indefinite	Varies; until change is required	5(f)
Fee imposed for permit	Yes (nominal)	No	No
Standards imposed on on non-point sources	No	No	Yes
Standards imposed on discharges to underground strata	Not permitted	Yes	Yes
Form of discharge standards	Concentration & quantity	Quantity	Quantity & % removal

a) Discharge must be reported to government. Permit is required for Osaka Prefecture.

b) For certain enterprises, only notification to the County Administration is necessary.

c) Normal duration indicated; any significant changes in enterprise require obtaining a new permit. In the Trent Basin, details of the permit may be changed after two years.

d) Concentration, example: mg/l; quantity, example: kilogrammes per day; % removal, example: 85% removal of BOD_5 from some base, often unspecified.

e) No discharge to underground from point sources is permitted.

f) Federal guidelines must be renewed every five years at least.

Table III-3

Factors Considered in Establishing Discharge Standards in Seven River Basins

Factors	River Basin						
	Trent (U.K.)	Parramatta (Australia)	Yodo (Japan)	Kavlingean (Sweden)	Dommel/Aa (Netherlands)	Seine/Nor. (France)	Delaware (U.S.)
Specific flow conditions	Yes	?	Yes	Yes	No	Yes	Yes
Existing ambient water quality-standards	Yes	?	Yes	–	Yes	Yes	Yes
Available technology	–	–	–	Yes	Yes	Yes	Yes
Variability in discharge (peak effects)	No	No	No	Yes	No	Yes	Yes(a)
Economic impact on discharger	Yes	Yes	Yes	Yes	No	Partially	Yes

a) Permits are generally written in terms of a 30-day mean and a maximum day in a 30-day period.

1. Discharge to Communal Facilities

The principal alternative to discharging residuals directly into water bodies is to discharge into communal facilities, such as a municipal sewerage system, in which the residuals are modified - or further modified - before discharge into water bodies or onto the land. Essentially the same types of discharge standards applied to direct discharges can be applied to discharges to communal facilities. Where such facilities include biological processes, particular attention is given to constituents which would "upset" the biological system. (This is analogous to the concern for discharges into water bodies which would upset natural ecosystems.) Thus, discharges of toxic m aterials are prohibited. Discharges of grease and oil are also likely to be prohibited, or severely limited.

Standards which have been applied to discharges into communal facilities include:

Limit on total wastewater quantity per day;
Limit on total quantity of various materials, e.g., kilogrammes of BOD_5, per day;
Limits on concentrations of various materials, e.g., BOD_5, phenols, suspended solids, cyanide, grease, oil;
Limit on pH; and
Limit on the variation inqquantity of wastewater, e.g., maximum instantaneous flow must be no more than 10 per cent larger than mean daily flow.

In the Trent, Dommel/Aa, Seine Normandy, Kävlingean and Yodo river basins, specific discharge standards are imposed on discharges into communal facilities. In the first three basins, these standards are imposed primarily by the river basin agencies; in the United States by a local agency, except where a regional agency is involved. Also in the United States, pre-treatment standards for such discharges are being developed at the national level, similar to the effluent (direct discharge) guidelines noted previously.

2. Concluding Comments

The following points are based on material submitted on the seven river basins:

1. Discharge standards based solely on concentration(s), unaccompanied by upper limits on total kilogrammes of discharges per day, can lead to overload of an aquatic ecosystem, because the ecosystem responds to total loads imposed on it, as well as to concentrations in discharges.

2. The form in which discharge standards - and/or effluent charges - are expressed in a permit to a discharger affects the associated monitoring provisions and procedures. (See Chapter V.B.)

3. In the United States, the reasonableness of discharge standards - or effluent charges if they existed - can be appealed to the judicial courts, which are distinct from administrative courts. A number of legal suits have been brought in connection with the effluent guidelines developed under the 1972 act, as well as with respect to conditions in individual discharge permits.

4. Discharges to ground water bodies are, in general, less easy to identify than discharges to surface water bodies. Once identified, complicated geohydrologic analyses are often necessary in order to determine what standards should be imposed on such discharges. Particularly difficult are discharges to ground waters from non-point (diffuse, dispersed, areal) sources, such as agricultural operations. Leaching into ground water from landfills (tips) and mine tailings sites can be identified, and applicable standards devised. However, implementation is often difficult with respect to tailings piles associated with mining operations which have been abandoned.

5. In establishing discharge standards in relation to ambient water quality standards, two approaches to providing a "margin of safety" are used. In the Seine/Normandie Basin, a margin of safety was achieved by using conservative values of coefficients in the Streeter-Phelps water quality model used to determine assimilative capacity, e.g., minimal re-aeration coefficients. In the Delaware Basin, procedures of the Delaware River Basin Commission require that a significant portion of the assimilative capacity be unallocated, as a reserve. This reserve provides some margin of safety with respect to inaccuracies in water quality modelling, inaccuracies in estimating discharges, and changes in activity levels and residuals generation over time.

6. In many, if not most, cases more stringent discharge standards are established for new activities than for existing activities, under the assumption that it is less costly for new activities to reduce discharges than it is for existing activities. Similarly, in some cases where different sections of a river or estuary have been allocated to different water uses, substantially different discharge standards have been established for a given type of activity. Such a procedure affects location decisions of enterprises.

7. Analysis of relative magnitudes of discharges from point and non-point sources has been carried out in only a few river basins. In the Delaware Basin, data available in 1962 at the beginning of

analyses leading to the establishment of discharge standards, indicated that point sources represented about three-quarters of the discharges of organic materials (as represented by BOD_5) and suspended solids. However, the data available were extremely limited, and did not include any consideration of washout phenomena. At present, in the Delaware as in other areas in the United States, planning studies are under way to determine to what extent reductions in discharges from non-point sources as well as from point sources are necessary to achieve ambient water quality standards.

8. Generally, permits to discharge are given for finite periods of time, ranging from one year (annual renewal required) to five years. Shorter time periods enable the results of a review of performance to be considered in permit renewal. Any basic changes in an activity generally require an application for a new permit.

Changes in permit conditions from one period to the next, e.g., tightening of discharge limits, should be considered no differently than changes in costs of other factor inputs, such as fuel, labour, other raw materials. If population and/or production continue to grow in a river basin in relation to the finite water resource, the price of the use of the assimilative capacity - as reflected in discharge standards - should increase to reflect the increased demand. The problem is to make the necessary changes in the discharge standards in a sequence which will minimise economic hardship. Any manager of an enterprise or of a communal treatment facility should recognise that the relative cost of discharging will very likely continue to increase in the future.

B. POLLUTION CHARGES

As already stated in the introduction of this chapter, pollution charges is a general term including both effluent charges, i.e., charges on direct discharges to water bodies, and user charges, i.e. charges paid for using collective treatment facilities. The common characteristic is that the payment is directly linked to the amount of pollutant discharged. Thus, when both effluent and user charges are used, as is the case in France and the Netherlands, the same principle and methods of calculation apply to both. When reference is made to pollution charges in the Seine-Normandy and Dommel/Aa river basins, it must be understood that it applies to both types of charges.

In all basins user charges are applied to discharges to communal treatment facilities. Effluent charges are imposed only in the Seine-Normandy and Dommel/Aa river basins. Consequently, the following paragraphs in this section are based mainly on information from the case studies of these basins.

1. Why should a system of pollution charges exist side by side with a system of emission standards?

Regulation thus very often does not suffice to lessen pollution. If public and private polluters do not allocate the necessary expenditure for effectively complying with the regulations, the slowness of legal proceedings, the small penalties imposed and the technical difficulty of determining the source of pollution often have the effect of preventing the authorities in practice from stemming the tide of pollution.

The introduction of a system of charges provides new financial resources supplementing those of the central government's budget. These funds will enable a programme for investing in (and sometimes also operating) pollution control devices to be launched, where no source of finance existed before.

Charges and action programmes are hence closely linked. Usually both sides balance out from a budgetary standpoint: in this event a redistributive charge is said to be involved.(1)

The regulations governing collection of the charge call for the multiplication of two terms in order to calculate the total amount:

- assessment of the amount of pollution generated or discharged, known as the basis for the charge;
- the price per unit of assessment basis, known as the rate of the charge.

The rate is obtained through economic calculation (for example by dividing the amount of investment under the programme to be undertaken by the total amount of pollution generated in the case of redistributive charges) or political calculation (how much are the polluters prepared to pay in order to abate the pollution?).

The assessment basis marks a step forward in regard to knowledge of the quantities and forms of pollution generated and discharged. Depending on the case, pollution can be assessed directly by measuring devices (in the event of very heavy pollution), or a flat-rate approach may be used by means of coefficients for converting observations easy to make (number of persons residing or working in some given locality, quantity or volume of manufactured goods produced during some unit of time).

---

1) Which should not be confused with the efficient charge (providing the incentive to cover operating and amortization costs) and with the optimal economic charge (with a rate equivalent to the marginal cost of damage), this latter being mentioned here only for reference. See Water Management Policies and Instruments, OECD 1977, §§ 4.2.1 and 4.2.2 and Pollution Charges: An Assessment, OECD 1976.

To sum up, the system of pollution charges enables:

- funds to be collected for pollution control without weighing on the State's pre-existing finances;
- new investment to be planned and the time-table to be scheduled;
- essential information on amounts of pollution generated and discharged to be obtained by means of the assessment basis.

These three advantages are linked through a simple arithmetic operation:

Let F be the investment programme (which may be annual or pluri-annual) to be covered by the charges F; A be the amount of pollution which can be assessed by measurement or by the flat-rate calculation method, and t be the financial rate of the charge. We then have:

$$R = F$$
$$R = At$$
$$t = \frac{F}{A}$$

If F is a pluri-annual investment programme (hence a forecast), the rate t will be of an estimated nature and will usually be corrected during implementation of the programme. If instead F involves annual expenditure, t will be fixed for one year and change each year.

If the system of pollution charges is compared with the more conventional system of emission standards, both may be regarded as adequately complementing each other. Far from being "rights to pollute" (since the standards remain applicable), the charges provide an effective means of observing compliance or non-compliance with the standards, owing to the information obtained at the time of evaluating the assessment bases. Moreover the financial resources collected through the charges enable the standards to be actually observed, as in cases where through lack of money the polluters are unable to comply with them without however entailing their disappearance (an extremely frequent case where municipalities - and not the smallest - are concerned, and one also arising in certain industries or agricultural activities). The charges enable indebtedness created by the introduction of rules regarding discharges to be spread more widely, both over time (case of pluri-annual investment programmes which can make up lags and compensate for increased pollution) and especially among polluters by using a new distribution key which differs from traditional bases of assessment (municipal, regional or federal), narrowly confined within a political system of careful control.

2. Determining the assessment basis of charges

Physical terms expressing the various types of water pollutant form the basis for assessing the charges.

Generally such physical factors are the following:

- suspended solids;
- oxidisable matter expressed by biochemical oxygen demand (BOD) or chemical oxygen demand (COD);
- nitrogenous substances reckoned according to the Kjeldahl formula;
- inhibiting and toxic substances;
- soluble salts.

More detailed indications appear in the Annex.

Usually these factors are combined and form "pollution assessment units" for which weighting and correction coefficients are used.

By means of these weighting coefficients it is possible to show, for example, the heavier cost of treating some particular from of pollution, or the threat it presents for the receptor medium's waste-assimilative capacity. Oxidisable matter will thus be assigned a heavier weighting coefficient than suspended solids, and toxic substances one greater than for oxidisable matter, etc. The correction coefficients particularly apply to the amounts of water used in discharging pollutants. A positive or negative correction may be introduced (as in the Dommel and Aa basin) in accordance with a predetermined volume standard. This serves as an incentive not to waste water.

As the charges are quantities expressed in absolute terms (monetary units), the assessment bases must be evaluated in terms of pollution flows and not concentrations of polluting substances.

The bases are therefore expressed in terms of kilogrammes of pollution per day or per year, or else convenient units of mass (e.g. in population-equivalents). In every case they are determined:

- either by direct measurement, by multiplying:
  - a) the figure obtained for the (daily or hourly) rate of discharge of the pollutant; and
  - b) the figure obtained for the average or instantaneous concentration (by sampling) in the flow
- or by evaluating by means of conversion coefficients, production units then being replaced by amounts of pollution (see Annex). A householder is thus "worth" 180 gr/day of pollution in the Netherlands and 147 gr/day in France. A worker in the chemical industry in the Netherlands is "worth" 20 population-equivalents, a worker in a French oil refinery is worth 3, etc.

Direct measurements are reserved for the heaviest pollution. The funds yielded by the charges in this case are largely used to cover the expense of the measurement operation (or operations if discharge is irregular). Such measurements moreover usually call for costly special installations (especially in calculating rates of discharge).

Flat-rate calculations apply to small polluting units. Usually these benefit the polluters to some extent, yet enable the pollution from small point sources to be adequately covered at minimum administrative cost. The flat-rate method of evaluation can progressively be replaced by actual measurement as needed in the case of the most significant sources.(1)

3. Calculating the rate of charge

In the Dommel and Aa basins the charges balance out with the yearly instalments of an investment programme, as clearly shown in the following tables:

Table III-4

COMPUTATION OF POLLUTION CHARGES
(1973 prices)

Dommel Waterboard

1973 Estimate of the Charge per Unit of Pollution for the Year 1977

	Investments Dfl. 10^6	Annual Expenses Dfl. 10^6
Trunk sewers	86.1	8.6
Treatment stations	155.5	22.5
Collecting Expenses	-	-
General Expenses	-	-
	246.1	33.1

Charge for a total load of 1.435×10^6 pollution units — Dfl. 23.- per p.e. $= \dfrac{33.1 \cdot 10^6}{1,435 \cdot 10^6}$

---

1) In the Seine-Normandy basin, a classification of pollution sources by order of importance shows that the 200 most heavily polluting industrial establishments account for 80 per cent of pollution, while the 1400 following merely account for the remaining 20 per cent.

Aa Waterboard

1973 Estimate of the Charge per Unit of Pollution for
the Year 1978

	Investments Dfl. 10^6	Annual Expenses Dfl. 10^6
Trunk sewers	23.6	2.6
Treatment stations	66.4	10.8
Collecting Expenses	-	0.7
General Expenses	-	0.7
	90.-	14.8

Charge for a total load of 0.63×10^6 pollution
units - Dfl. 23.40 per p.e. $= \dfrac{14.8 \; 10^6}{0.63 \; 10^6}$

In the Seine-Normandy basin the same sort of balance is achieved
between financial commitments and charges, but as it is pluri-annual
and several types of pollution are involved (hence several bases expressed in terms of different units), it is more complex.

Table III-5

SEINE-NORMANDY BASIN

1975 Estimate for 1976-1981 action programme

millions of 1975 francs

CONVENTIONAL POLLUTION	Amount for assisted work	Commit-ments	of which:		
			Subsi-dies	Loans	Advances
Local authorities (stations, collectors, networks)	2 176.8	643.4	540	64.4	39
Industrial stations	576	286.8	160.3	116.1	10.4
Elimination of sludge	52	24	24	-	-
Technical assistance	109	51.3	40	-	11.3
Measurements, quality objectives	74	46.6	44.6	2	-
Technological studies	94.8	51.7	51.7	-	-
VARIOUS INHIBITING SUBSTANCES	700	352.9	262.7	90.2	-
Bonuses to local authori-ties for treatment	-	1 016.4	1 016.4	-	-
Incentives for maximum pollution abatement	-	244.4	244.4	-	-
TOTAL	3 782.6	2 717.5	2 384.1	272.7	60.7

Amounts in this table allow for programme reductions made necessary
by government measures taken in 1977 to control inflation.

Balancing the charges (see Annex) leads to the following rates (orders of magnitude):

Table III-6

SEINE-NORMANDY BASIN

1975 Estimate for pollution charges under the
1976-1981 action programme

(PE)	1977 and 1978	Beyond 1979
Population equivalent(1)	10.00 F	11.55 F
SS (kg/day)	48.00 F	56.62 F
OM (kg/day)	96.00 F	113.24 F
Inhibiting substance (equitox)	1.00 F	1.15 F
Salinity ($\frac{mho}{cm}$ x m^3/day)	13.50 F	13.50 F

1) With OM = 2 SS.

. In 1977 government measures to limit price increases led to the adoption of a basic rate of Frs.8.26 per PE, Frs.40.47/kg/day for SS, Frs.80.94/kg/day for OM and Frs.0.852/equitox (no change for salinity, which in 1977 was subjected to no increase).

It should be noted that calculation of the rates for the Seine-Normandy basin is based on a forecast of an expenditure programme. Two risks of error may thus arise: a wrong estimate of the future assessment basis (i.e. the future quantity of polluting discharges), and an inaccurate estimate of future expenditure to be covered (i.e. the amount of work to be achieved).

The significant disparity between the amount of charges in the Netherlands (Dommel and Aa basins) and in France (Seine-Normandy basin) will be noted, the latter being some four times smaller than the former.

4. Redistribution of revenue from charges

Tables III-5 and III-7 show how charges are redistributed.

Redistribution may be complete (as in the Dommel and Aa basins, where charges cover 100 per cent of pollution control expenditures) or partial (as in the Seine-Normandy basin, where commitments only account for 70 per cent of the amount allocated to assisted projects on average).

Actually such partial intervention considerably varies, depending on the kind of operation. A distinction should thus be made between investment expenditure financed on average to the tune of 45 per cent by the Seine-Normandy Basin Agency (Table III-5)

and the operating expenditure of treatment plants, for which agency
assistance may widely differ following complex calculations (see
Annex).

Table III-7

REDISTRIBUTION OF CHARGES IN THE SEINE-NORMANDY BASIN

	Financial aids provided			
Capital transactions (investment)	Industries		Municipalities	
	Subsidy	Loan	Subsidy	Loan
River basin agency subsidy	30%		30%	
River basin agency loan or advance		20%		10%
State subsidy	0		30%	
"Region" or "département" subsidy	0		10%	
Balance to be covered by self-financing or borrowing		50% (loan on commercial bank terms)		20% (loan on terms of major public financing institutions)
for Total investment to be financed		100% (of which 70% to be repaid)		100% (of which 30% to be repaid)

5. Computing the charges for discharges by industry and discharges by municipalities

The main factors in computing charges have been described in
section 2. In the Annex additional information is provided for actual detailed calculation. Two examples concerning industrial establishments (a tannery and an oil refinery) moreover give some idea of
how the rules for calculation in force can be used (application of
pre-determined flat rates; allowing for measurements where conversion coefficients are used).

Calculation of the charge to be paid by a municipality is also
shown in the Annex. It is not complex, merely requiring a knowledge
of the number of inhabitants in a commune's built-up area. A rate
(which may be adjusted according to the size of commune in the Seine-
Normandy basin) is then applied.

In the case of the Netherlands' Dommel and Aa basins, the rate
may be financially broken down according to the various costs which
must be borne:

Table III-8

1975 ESTIMATES: COMPONENTS OF UNIT COST
OF POLLUTION ABATEMENT

District	Load in p.e.	Investment	Other expenses	Administration	Government charges	TOTAL
		Unit cost in Fl/p.e.				
Dommel	1.650	7.36	4.70	1.39	–	13.45
Aa	630	6.30	4.21	3.03	–	13.54
Estimates for 1985						
Dommel	1.625	13.77	13.51	5.64	–	32.92
Aa	610	12.09	14.77	7.99		34.85

The investment column refers to the amortization of existing
installations and the building of new ones.

"Other expenses" cover the cost of operating treatment plants,
sewer systems and pumping stations (maintenance and operating costs).

Under "Administration" are listed the operating costs of management services and technical studies.

In certain cases (other than those of the Dommel Aa basin) an
additional charge must be paid into the national authority for the
amount of uneliminated pollution discharged into surface waters under
the jurisdiction of the national government.

The assumption that the polluting load to be treated will not
vary will be noted for purposes of calculating the rates.

6. Have charges been established for underground discharges?

In the Netherlands the system described above has not been extended to underground discharges. In France such discharges are
usually controlled, i.e. kept down to a minimum. To this end the
charges on pollution through infiltration (especially when produced
by the cesspool system) are increased by 50 per cent (see section 8
below).

It should be noted that by knowing the quantities of water abstracted (from the abstraction charges levied) and the quantities of
waste water discharged (from the pollution charges) it is possible
to obtain approximate figures for estimating how much water is lost,
in particular through clandestine underground discharge. These calculations have become more methodical thanks to recent attempts in
France to make mathematical models of the water economy in the Oise
River Basin, enabling hitherto little known underground discharges
to be located.

7. Charges and non-point discharges (municipal, industrial, mining and agricultural)

By definition, non-point sources are those for which the discharges are dispersed, rather than concentrated at one or more readily identifiable locations. Non-point sources can usefully be divided into non-urban and urban. The former includes such activities as agricultural, mining, and forest products; the latter is urban storm run-off.

With respect to non-urban sources, there is a range in the degree to which residuals discharges can be associated with particular non-point activities. For example, the boundaries and characteristics of a mine tailings pile, an agricultural operation, and a management unit of a forest can be delineated. Substantial experience has been accumulated in the United States in the use of empirical formulae for estimating residuals generation by such activities. Some variation of the "Universal Soil Loss Equation" is the most commonly used. The results of its application are probably no less accurate than the tables used to estimate discharges by industrial operations without measurements.

Given that discharges from these non-urban non-point sources can be estimated, then either effluent charges or effluent standards can be imposed. The basis for the payment, or the determination of compliance or non-compliance with standards, would be based on the discharge estimated. Reduction in discharge would be achieved by the adoption by the discharger of various physical measures, such as construction of terraces and grassed waterways by a farmer. The other approach to controlling non-urban non-point sources is by specification of best management practices, as discussed in Section III.A.

With respect to urban storm run-off, in most urban areas the run-off is eventually channelled into storm sewers or storm channels, which discharge at readily identifiable points into water bodies. In effect, the dispersed origin of the run-off (discharge) has become a point source. As such, it could be subject to effluent standards or charges just as other types of point sources. The responsible municipality could then impose various regulations on individual activities within the municipality to reduce run-off.

8. Rates of charge according to district

In the Netherlands the rates of charge are the same along both rivers (the Dommel and the Aa) in the river concerned, but not in France, where a rather complicated system is used.

There are three possible systems:

- the first (chosen by the Netherlands) is the most satisfactory, at least in appearance, as regards equity, since it
  consists in levying a uniform charge with a particular district regardless of where the polluting source may be(1);
- the second consists in varying the rates of charge by raising
  them where the quantities of pollutants discharges are
  greater, which usually means higher charges the farther down
  the river basin. In this case polluters near the source of
  a watercourse bear little if any of the expenditure on controlling pollution in the estuary. Concentration was the
  most serious factor in the emergence of pollution and is the
  factor most penalised by this system;
- the third system (chosen by France in the example given in
  this paper) is the opposite of the preceding one. It calls
  for protection of the areas upstream, where higher rates of
  charge should be applied, while the rates in the areas downstream and in the estuary should be lower because the large-
  scale drainage and waste treatment facilities there enable
  economies of scale to be made, and also a higher assimilative
  capacity.

If 1 (the base rate) be the coefficient applied in the lower
reaches and estuaries of watercourses, the following are the increases made according to area (Table III-9).

The charge on salinity is in practice applied only to part of
area No. 3 (the estuary in the wider sense).

The coefficients are also changed for rivers or sections of
rivers covered by a Decree on quality objectives (see Section II,
as follows (Table III-10), to the extent of 50 per cent of the base
rate.

9. Rates of charge by districts and industrial development

While the impact of the charges (which seems less severe in
this respect than strict controls) is a sufficient deterrent to setting up new industrial plants, the foregoing tables show that in the
Seine-Normandy Basin:

- industrial development is encouraged to some extent in the
  lower reaches and in the estuary, i.e. where it already
  exists;

---

1) Notable differences (as much as a two-to-one ratio) may exist
   between various districts. The Dommel and Aa charges may be
   regarded as being in the lower bracket of those applying in the
   forty some districts involved.

Table III-9

AREA COEFFICIENTS USED IN THE SEINE-NORMANDY BASIN
FOR ADJUSTING POLLUTION CHARGE RATES (MULTIPLIERS)

Areas	Suspended solids	Oxidisable matter	Inhibiting substances
1			
. Upstream, low density of population and industrialisation	1.5	1.5	1
. Discharges by infiltration	1.5	1.5	1.5
. Coastal shellfish-breeding area	1.5	1.5	1.5
2			
. Inland waters, middle reaches (average density)	1.2	1.2	1
. Discharges by infiltration	1.2	1.2	1.5
. Bathing area, discharge into the estuary zone	1.5	1.2	1.5
. Bathing area, discharge offshore beyond the estuary zone	1.2	1	1.5
3			
. Lower reaches and estuary (reference base)	1	1	1
. Discharges by infiltration	1	1	1.5

Table III-10

MULTIPLIER COEFFICIENTS APPLIED TO BASE RATE OF POLLUTION
CHARGES TO QUALITY-OBJECTIVE AREAS IN REGARD TO SURFACE
WATER (Seine-Normandy basin)

	Suspended solids	Oxidisable matter	Inhibiting substances	Salt
Quality-objective area	1.5	1.5	1.5	unchanged

- it is not encouraged in the upper reaches or coastal bathing areas;
- it is not encouraged along rivers with stretches governed by Decrees on quality objectives, whether these stretches are upstream or downstream.

The policy implied here may be contrasted with the policy implemented by strict controls in the lower reaches of the River Yodo in Japan (downstream from Kyoto), where industrial development is largely arrested because of overconcentration.

In other words, in a comparable area (the lower reaches of a river) industrial development is made very difficult in one case, but is allowed to proceed in the other.

Actually these regional planning considerations should be compared in the light of the waste-treatment technology to be used and of the residual assimilative capacity of the natural receptor medium.

In situations where the best technology (which is economically practicable) is used in highly industrialised areas, the receptor medium's assimilative capacity will often reach saturation point.

One solution that favours urban and industrial development and can be used in such hydrographic basins is to space out the factories and settlements along the watercourses. This is the solution chosen for the Yodo. It enables maximum use to be made of assimilative capacity by transferring new factories, settlements, etc. from the overcrowded sectors to the less crowded sectors.

A second solution is to make new activities choose sites outside the basin by refusing to expand it any further.

A third solution is to decide to lower the quality of the environment. Better technology (which usually costs more) may postpone this decision and even obviate it. In the Seine-Normandy Basin the levying of higher charges in critical zones (governed by Decree on minimum quality objectives) is used as a means of obtaining more funds for developing a more advanced technology.

10. Incentive effect of charges

This subject is developed in annex "D". If the cost of maintaining and operating treatment plants is taken as reference, the charge has an incentive effect in the Dommel and Aa basins since it largely exceeds operating expenditure (see Table III-8 above). By means of the aid for maximum pollution abatement and in protected areas (upstream and bathing areas or quality-objective areas), in the Seine-Normandy Basin the incentive level is approached.

Satisfactory though the incentive effect may be, it is only partial. The reference used (operating cost with the best practicable technology) may be misleading for several reasons:

- The incentive effect is not enough to promote the use of an
available technology that is more advanced and therefore more
costly (more efficient treatment of suspended solids and oxidisable matter, removal of nitrogenous substances and phosphorus, suppression of toxic elements and heavy metals, and
disinfection of residual wastes).
- The economic reference base chosen (operating costs are related entirely to technology) does not take account of damage
caused by pollution to the natural environment, especially
biological and ecological damage.

While the economic incentive provided by levying charges would
seem to be an excellent short- and medium-term solution, it should
not be regarded as a universal panacea for all environmental ail-
ments, and the same common-sense remark might be made with reference
to the controls now imposed on polluters.

11. Programme for the regular upgrading of charges

The goal of making charges more incentive by progressively increasing the rates is one sought both in the Netherlands (Dommel and
Aa basins) and France (Seine-Normandy Basin).

The report by the Central Financial Auditing and Advisory Bureau
on the study of pollution charges thus shows such a pregression
(Table III-11).

Table III-11

ANNUAL POLLUTION CHARGES LEVIED (1971-1974) AND ESTIMATES
OF FUTURE CHARGES (1975-1980) IN THE VARIOUS DISTRICTS

Unit charge Fl/p.e.

	Dommel district	Aa district
1971	5.20	3
1972	7	3.50
1973	9	5.80
1974	11	8.60
1975	13	10.68
1976	18	17.04
1977	23.04	22.32
1978	25.92	25.25
1979	29	25
1980	32	24.75

In the Seine-Normandy basin the rates are fixed when the action programmes of the basin financing agencies are drawn up. These programmes usually cover the same five-year periods as the national Plans (Sixth Plan: 1971-1975; Seventh Plan: 1976-1980, etc.).

Base rates as observed and forecast in the Seine-Normandy basin are as follows:

Table III-12

TREND IN RATES OF POLLUTION CHARGES IN THE SEINE-NORMANDY BASIN

Francs/population-equivalent

		Base rates
1st programme	1969	1.12
	1970	1.69
2nd programme	1971	2.25
	1972	3.75
	1973	4.41
	1974	4.41
	1975	4.41
Intermediate programme	1976	7.72
3rd programme	1977	8.26
(estimates)	1978	10
"	1979	11.55
"	1980	11.55
	1981	11.55

These increases only partly allow for readjustments necessitated by monetary erosion (see section 12 below). They are however closely related to long-term pollution abatement objectives, including the lage to be made up in controlling pollution while also dealing with rising pollution due to urban and industrial growth. A diagram of the programming process appears in the Annex.

12. Charges and the erosion of money

The effects of inflation on efficiency of the charge are partially allowed for.

In the Dommel and Aa basins corrective indices are used in estimating the trend for charges (see Table III-8 above).

Investment expenditure: 7 per cent price index change per year from 1975

Operating expenditure: 12 per cent price index change in 1976 over 1975
8 per cent price index change in 1977 over 1976

7 per cent price index change after
1977

Administrative expenditure: 7 per cent price index from 1975.

In the Seine-Normandy basin, account is taken periodically of
the erosion of money, namely when the pluri-annual action programmes
are drawn up. But an adjustment is not made systematically every
year, and lowered efficiency of the charges is noted at the end of
each programme (see Table III-12). Under the first two programmes,
for example, the charges corrected for changes in the index of
building and contracting costs is as follows:

Table III-13

EFFECT OF INFLATION ON RATES OF CHARGE

	Rate of charge in francs at current prices	Rate of charge corrected for building and contracting price index
1969	1.12	1.12
1970	1.69	1.54
1971	2.25	1.87
1972	3.75	2.81
1973	4.41	2.82
1974	4.41	2.30
1975	4.41	2.04

13. Rates of charge for new polluters

In the Dommel-Aa as in the Seine-Normandy basins new polluters
and existing polluters are charged the same rates. As regards sta-
tutory controls, however, new installations must meet strict discharge standards. Charges applying only to residual pollution,
therefore logically are low.

Chapter IV

ESTABLISHMENT OF ABSTRACTION (WITHDRAWAL) CONTROLS

A. LICENSES

In order to control the exploitation of water resources, some countries adopt regulations whereby raw water may be abstracted directly from water bodies only under license. This procedure can serve one or more purposes. At a minimum, a system of licenses (permits) for abstractions is the means by which a water resources management agency maintains an inventory of abstractions. In addition, a license can specify the conditions under which the abstraction can take place and the payment, if any, to be made for the abstraction. (Rationales for abstraction charges are discussed in Section IV.B.) Table IV-1 lists the types of conditions which may be contained in a license.

Table IV.1

POSSIBLE LICENSE (PERMIT) CONDITIONS FOR WATER ABSTRACTIONS

Limit on rate of abstraction, cubic meters/second:

  a) No restriction by time of year;
  b) With seasonal restriction;
  c) With restriction under specified flow conditions

Limit on total quantity of abstraction per day, per week, per year, or combinations of these time periods

Period of time for which license is in effect

Conditions requiring reapplication for license, e.g., change in level of production, change in production process

Limit on transferability of license, e.g. can or cannot be transferred to another water user and under what conditions

Specification that abstraction must be measured continuously with specified degree of accuracy and results reported periodically to management agency, or specification of information to be made available to enable estimates of abstractions to be made in lieu of direct measurements

Schedule or basis of charges for abstractions

Material submitted with respect to licensing of abstractions in the seven river basins is summarised in Table IV-2. In addition to the information in the table, the following points can be made.

1) In all seven basins, some type of abstraction license is required. Licensing of ground water abstractions is less common than licensing of surface water abstractions.

2) In virtually all cases where an abstraction license system exists, some exemptions are permitted, either because of the nature of the water use or the size of the abstraction or both. To illustrate, the following types of abstractions are exempted in the **Severn-Trent River Basin:**

- Abstraction from ground water for domestic purposes in the abstractor's household;
- Abstraction for general agricultural and farm use (excluding spray irrigation) from surface waters adjacent to the farm;
- Abstraction of less than 5 m^3;
- Abstraction for land drainage purposes;
- Abstraction to prevent interference with mining, quarrying, engineering, or building operations;
- Abstraction from an inland water by a Navigation Authority; and
- Abstraction of water for fire fighting.

3) In the United Kingdom and Japan, obtaining a license for abstraction is a process which includes careful appraisal by governmental authorities, announcement and publication of the conditions of the proposed abstraction, and provision for objections by other water users.

4) The water law of a country can have a major impact on the establishment of abstraction controls. For example, in Japan, ground water is legally owned by the overlying landowner; therefore it is not subject to government regulation **except those to prevent ground subsidence.**

B. ABSTRACTION CHARGES

Of the seven cases discussed in this paper only four, Seine-Normandy, Yodo, Trent and Delaware River basins, have established a system of charges on water abstractions (withdrawals). The Parramatta, Kävlingean and Dommel/Aa basins do not use such a system. In the case of the Dommel/Aa basin, a water control charge is however collected on issuing an abstraction licence. This is a levy demanded by the Water Board to recoup the expenses incurred in the quantity

Table IV.2

LICENSING PROVISIONS RELATING TO WATER ABSTRACTIONS IN SEVEN RIVER BASINS

	Trent (U.K.)	Parramatta (Australia)	Yodo (Japan)	Kavlingean (Sweden)
License required for abstractions:				
from surface water	Y	Y	Y	Y
from ground water	Y	Y	N	Y
Some activities exempted, e.g., either no license or no fee required or both	Y	?	N	Y
Allowable abstraction specified as: capacity of facility,				
size of farm	-	Y	Y	N
flow rate	-	-	-	Y
total per hour, max.	Y	-	-	(a)
total per day, max.	Y	-	Y	(a)
total per year, max.	Y	-	Y	(a)
Allowable abstraction varied:				
by season	-	N	Y (for drought)	Y
by flow conditions	Y	N	Y (for drought)	Y
Duration of license, years:				
surface water	Indefinite(b)	5(c)	30/10(d)	Indefinite(e)
ground water	5	5(c)	-	Indefinite(e)
Fee imposed for license:				
surface water	Y	Y	N	N
ground water	Y	N	-	N
annual fee	Y	Y	-	N
per unit fee	-	Y	-	N
Priorities among users established	Y	Y	N	-

	Dommel/Aa (Netherlands)	Seine/Nor. (France)	Delaware (U.S.)
License required for abstractions:			
from surface water	Y	Y	Y
from ground water	Y	Y	?
Some activities exempted, e.g., either no license or no fee required or both	N (surface water) Y (ground water)	Y	Y
Allowable abstraction specified as: capacity of facility,			
size of farm	(f)	N	-
flow rate	Y	N	?
total per hour, max.	-	N	-
total per day, max.	Y (per ten days)	Y	?
total per year, max.	Y	Y	-
Allowable abstractions varied:			
by season	N	Y (for drought)	N
by flow conditions	Y	Y (for drought)	N
Duration of license, years:			
surface water	Indefinite	Indefinite	?
ground water	Indefinite	Indefinite	?
Fee imposed for license:			
surface water	Y (nominal)	N	N
ground water	Y (nominal)	N	N
annual fee	N	N	-
per unit fee	N	N	-
Priorities among users established	N	N (except in drought)	Y?

a) Different in different cases.
b) With few exceptions where time limits are imposed.
c) Except 10 years for public water supplies.
d) Thirty years for hydroelectric energy generation; ten years for all other.
e) Can be specified in license.
f) Surface water abstractions are primarily for agricultural and horticultural purposes. Allowable abstraction rate for horticultural use is higher than for agricultural use.

management of the surface waters of the region. In the area
controlled by the Water Boards of the River Aa and River Dommel the
charges per dwelling vary between Fl.15.- and Fl.20.- per annum.(1)
In the Parramatta Basin there is also a fee which depends on the
extent of the irrigated area. It accompanies a licence to abstract
valid for 15 years thus:

50 l/s or 4 ha irrigated: Aust.$72 (i.e., US$15.65 per year)
or 1 cent/1000m^3/s

230 l/s or 30 ha irrigated: $189 (i.e., US$41 per year) or
0.56 cent/1000m^3/s

162 ha irrigated: $558 (i.e., US$121.3 per year).

For recreational uses of water or urban uses (drinking water)
the fee is Aust.$60 (i.e. US$6.5 per year, because in this case the
licence is valid for 10 years).

However, there are signs that an abstraction charge is emerging.
In order to meet the expense of maintaining the control works on the
Parramatta River a charge for services rendered (and not for water
use) is paid to the Water Resources Commission of New South Wales,
amounting to 28 cents/1000m^3 ($\frac{US\$0.30}{1000}/_m3$).

Cases for the other basins (Seine-Normandy, Yodo, Trent and
Delaware) are more complex, and are described in the following
pages.

1. Calculation of abstraction charges

Abstraction charges are imposed in some of the countries
studied on direct withdrawals from the natural environment. Charges
may be imposed on the total abstraction, as in France, or on the
quantity above a free allowance. Various exemptions and conditions
exist. For example, a notable case of exemption from abstraction
charges is New York City, which is entitled to withdraw water free
of charge from the upper reaches of the Delaware River, but in

---

1) The exchange rates used in this study are shown in the annex to
   Chapter III:

Exchange rates for $1(U.S.) (1976 period)

       0.92 Australian dollar
       4.97 French francs
   293.00 Yen
       2.46 Dutch guilder
       4.37 Swedish crown
       0.587 Pound

return must guarantee a minimum flow in the river.(1) Water is
also diverted from the Delaware Basin to New Jersey, also without
payment and with no provisions for compensating releases. In Japan
only hydropower stations and industrial activities pay the charges;
abstractions for public utility or irrigation purposes are exempted
or are charged at much lower rates. In the United Kingdom a consumption factor raises the charge on uses involving loss of water,
as in irrigation, and lowers it on uses involving minimum loss,
i.e., washing building materials and open-circuit cooling for power
stations. Thus, generally speaking, it is the industrial uses or
large abstractions for water supply purposes (except in Japan)
which pay charges. For irrigation there is special treatment
consisting either of exempting it, lowering the charge, or granting
free allowances (as in the Delaware River Basin and Japan), or in
applying special rules which allow for loss of water by evapo-
transpiration (as in France and the United Kingdom).

As a rule, only large quantities of water are counted. There
is a minimum threshold of 6000 m^3/year in France, while in the
Delaware River Basin the only abstractions charged are those which
exceed the water allowances laid down in "certificates of entitle-
ment" in 1961 or the quantities abstracted in 1971 (in the absence
of a "certificate").

The origin and usefulness of these charges (which theoretically
are incentives for making efficient use of water) are to be found in
the amortization of large water control or supply works. In the
Delaware River Basin the charges are used for repaying expenditure
incurred for building federal multipurpose storage dams, and are
levied only in sections of the river affected by the latter. In the
Yodo basin the financial use of the charges is not so clear-cut; new
abstractors may have to pay additional charges depending on the
increased demand which they generate.

In the Seine-Normandy basin the charges help to finance an aid
programme described below (Table IV.3 and Figure IV.1). The charges
cover the commitments and the financial balancing item in the programme (see Section III.B3: Calculating the rate of charge).
Figure IV.1 shows the type of accounting balance. Revenue is
obtained by applying various charge rates (detailed below) to an
assessment basis calculated in cubic metres. (Charges are therefore
expressed in francs/m^3). Water demand is measured by water, electric,
or time meters which are read by the abstractor under the supervision

---

1) Except during dry periods, when restrictions are negotiated.

Table IV.3

PROGRAMME 1977-1981 FOR QUANTITATIVE IMPROVEMENT
OF WATER RESOURCES (Seine-Normandy River Basin)

Operations	Francs million	
	Cost of assisted works (investment)	Financial Agency commitments
- Protection of ground water	205 (M$ 41.2)	120 (M$ 24.1)
- Large dams and raising of low water level	120 (M$ 24.1)	95 (M$ 19.1)
- Interconnections between water supply systems and safeguarding of supplies in the Greater Paris Area	330 (M$ 66.4)	150 (M$ 30.2)
- Major transfers of water within the Basin	375 (M$ 75.4)	143 (M$ 28.8)
- Planning and miscellaneous	45 (M$ 9)	32 (M$ 6.4)
- Meters for measuring abstractions	6 (M$ 1.2)	6 (M$ 1.2)
	1081 (M$ 217.5)	546 (M$ 109.8)

of government representatives. If there is no meter, estimates may
be made (which are usually unfavourable to the abstractor); they are
based on the physical features of the industrial process or other
activity and on the performance and operating times of pumps. Some
estimates concern particular activities such as agriculture
(irrigation) and gravel pit operations in excavations, water-logged
conditions, or rivers.

2. Rates of charge and categories of abstractor

All countries which use a system of abstraction charges distinguish different categories of abstractor.

In the Yodo basin the main distinction is between mining and
industrial activity, hydropower production, and supplies of drinking
water to towns (the latter being practically exempt from the charge).
The highest rates of charge are applied to industrial activities,
and the rates increase from the estuary of a river towards its
source (Table IV.4).

Figure 4.1

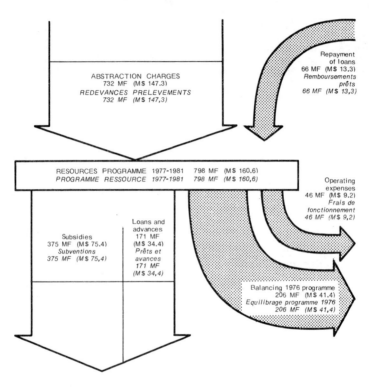

REDISTRIBUTION OF ABSTRACTION CHARGES
(SEINE-NORMANDY)
*REDISTRIBUTION DU PRODUIT DES REDEVANCES
DE PRELEVEMENT (SEINE-NORMANDIE)*

ABSTRACTION CHARGES
732 MF (M$ 147.3)
*REDEVANCES PRELEVEMENTS
732 MF (M$ 147,3)*

Repayment
of loans
66 MF (M$ 13.3)
*Remboursements
prêts
66 MF (M$ 13,3)*

RESOURCES PROGRAMME 1977-1981 798 MF (M$ 160.6)
PROGRAMME RESSOURCE 1977-1981 798 MF (M$ 160,6)

Operating
expenses
46 MF (M$ 9.2)
*Frais de
fonctionnement
46 MF (M$ 9,2)*

Subsidies
375 MF (M$ 75.4)
*Subventions
375 MF (M$ 75,4)*

Loans and
advances
171 MF
(M$ 34.4)
*Prêts et
avances
171 MF
(M$ 34,4)*

Balancing 1976 programme
206 MF (M$ 41.4)
*Equilibrage programme 1976
206 MF (M$ 41,4)*

MF : millions francs
M$: millions dollars

72

Table IV.4

EXAMPLES OF ABSTRACTION CHARGE RATES IN THE YODO BASIN

Prefecture	Industrial and mining activities	Other uses
Osaka area (lower Yodo) tidal section (estuary)	¥ 200/1/s (UScent $\frac{2}{1000}$ /m³/year)	¥ 200/1/s (US cent $\frac{2}{1000}$ /m³/year)
Non-tidal section	Abstraction <100 1/s ¥ 1600/1/s ($\frac{17}{1000}$ cent/m³/year) Abstraction >100 1/s ¥ 3200/1/s ($\frac{33}{1000}$ cent/m³/year)	Abstraction <100 1/s ¥ 1600/1/s ($\frac{17}{1000}$ cent/m³/year) Abstraction >100 1/s ¥ 3200 1/s ($\frac{33}{1000}$ cent/m³/year)
Kyoto area (middle Yodo)	¥ 2000/1/s ($\frac{20}{1000}$ cent/m³/year)	¥ 500/1/s ($\frac{5}{1000}$ cent/m³/year)
Shiga area (upper Yodo)	¥ 3150/1/s ($\frac{32}{1000}$ cent/m³/year)	¥ 2100/1/s ($\frac{22}{1000}$ cent/m³/year)

The charges indicated in yen are annual (unlike the French Taxes and those of the Delaware Basin, which apply to each m³ abstracted). They are converted into US cents and reduced for 1 m³ abstracted during one year (the rate used is 292 yen = 1 US$ (1976).

There is a special formula for abstractions to be used by power stations:

charge (in yen) = 1160 n + 256 (m-n)

where n = nominal theoretical output in kilowatts

m = theoretical maximum output

(in the case of hydropower stations without pumped storage).

One can also have:

charge (in yen) = $\sqrt{1160 n + 256 (m-n)}$ k (1)

where k is a correction factor for the proportion of output obtained by using pumped storage (k < 1).

The revenue from these various charges in 1975 was as follows (Table IV.5).

Table IV.5

REVENUE FROM ABSTRACTION CHARGES IN YODO BASIN, 1975
(THOUSANDS OF YEN)

Prefecture	Electric power generation	Industrial and mining uses	Other uses and town supplies	Total
Osaka area (downstream)	293 (US$1000)	10678 (US$36500)	88 ($300)	11059 (6%) ($37800)
Kyoto area	91516	273	181 (of which town supplies 4)	91970 (49%) ($314000)
Shiga area (upstream)	73897	7381	1618	82896 (45%) ($283000)
River Yodo	165706 (M$0.56) (89%)	18332 ($62000) (10%)	1887 ($6500) (1%)	185925 (M$0.63) (100%)

M$ = millions of US dollars

In the Seine-Normandy basin a distinction is made between abstraction (when the water is returned after use) as practised mainly by industries and consumption (when only some of the water is returned) as found in certain industrial activities, agriculture, town water supplies (in part) and electric power generation (evaporation from an expanse of water or cooling tower). Consumption usually costs more than abstraction, although this applies more to ground water (discussed later in paragraph 6) than to surface water.

----

1) Assuming that the difference between maximum and nominal output is 5 per cent, the maximum charge will be 1172.8 yen on $4 per KW.

Table IV.6

EXAMPLES OF ABSTRACTION CHARGE RATES IN THE SEINE-NORMANDY BASIN

(in 1977 centimes)

Region	Abstraction of surface water (industries and towns) (amount of water abstracted returned after use)		Consumption of surface water (1977) (electricity, agriculture and towns) (water not returned after use)	
	from 1st June to 30th October	from 1st November to 31st May	from 1st June to 30th October	from 1st November to 21st May
Upper Seine	0	0	3,727 ct/m³ (US ct.75/m³)	0
Reims (upstream of Oise-Aisne basin)	0	0	3,195 ct/m³ (US ct.64/m³)	0
Centre of basin				
– Above Paris				
• direct discharge	0.213 ct/m³ (US ct.04/m³)	0	0	0
• discharge into public sewers	7,455 ct/m³ (US ct.1.5/m³)	1 ct/m³ (US ct.0.2/m³)	0	0
– Below Paris	0,032 ct/m³ (US ct.0006/m³)	0	0	0
Lower Seine Le Havre	6,922 ct/m³ (US ct.1.4/m³)	6,922	0	0

The rates of charge depend mainly on the conditions of supply and demand on the local water market. In the example chosen (see Table IV.6) the rates tend to increase as one proceeds downstream along the Oise and the Seine (i.e. the opposite to what they do on the Yodo). It will be noted that abstraction charges for the Seine vary according to season, and that they are highest in summer, during low-water periods. Similarly, charges for the Trent are higher at low water (and smaller for more variable flow rates, as later shown in Table IV.8).

A breakdown of the revenue from these charges by categories of use show how the latter are affected. The following breakdown was calculated for 1974 (in millions of francs):

Table IV.7

REVENUE FROM ABSTRACTION CHARGES IN THE
SEINE-NORMANDY BASIN, 1974 (F MILLION)

Electric power generation	Town supplies			Irrigation	TOTAL
	Industrial uses	Munici-palities	Water supply undertakings		
2	21	22,5	34,2	0,1	79.8
(M$ 0,4)	(M$ 4,2)	(M$ 4.5)	(M$ 6.8)	(M$ 0.02)	(M$16)
2.5%	25.5%	71%		< 1%	100%

M$ = millions of US dollars

Here again, unlike in the Yodo basin, town water supplies account for most (70 per cent) of the revenue, while the charges on electric power generation are low.

In the Delaware River Basin in the United States a distinction is made between water consumed (charged at US ct.4/1000 gallons or about US ct.1.6/m^3) and water abstracted and returned, on which the charge is only one hundredth as much (US ct.0.016/m^3). Charges are not levied on the lower reaches of Delaware Bay, where salinisation is noticeable. In the intermediate zone between fresh water and salt water proportional charges are levied.

In the United Kingdom there is a formula for correcting the level of charges depending on the type of water supply, the quality of the water, the category of use and the time of year:

charge = T x Q x S x U x X p/m^3

where X is the base rate in pence/m^3.

Overall results are shown in Table IV.9.

Table IV.8

FACTORS USED FOR ADJUSTING CHARGES PER ABSTRACTION IN THE TRENT BASIN

T (Type of supply)		Q (Water quality)		U (Category of use)		S (Seasonal Factor)	
Releases from storage dams and inter-basin transfers	2	Good $NH_3 < 0.5mg/1$	1	Spray irrigation and cooling by evaporation	1	Low water	2
Flow boosted periodically	1	Average $0.5 < NH_3 < 3$	0.5	Industry and town supplies	0.4	Spate	0.2
Natural flow	0.5	Poor $NH_3 > 3mg/1$	0.25	Washing alluvium and open circuit cooling	0.02	Other periods	1
				Hydropower	0.001		

Table IV.9

ABSTRACTION CHARGES IN THE SEVERN-TRENT BASIN
(1977-1978 FINANCIAL YEAR)

in pence per 1000 gallons per year
Basic rate: 4.741 p/1000 gallons/year
$(1.044 \ p/m^3)$ $(1.77 \ US \ cts/m^3)$

		CATEGORY OF USE								
Source Availability	Source Quality	Spray Irrigation and Evaporated Cooling Water			Industrial, Public Water Supply & Misc.			Sand and Gravel Washing and Circulated Cooling Water		Water Power
		Summer Only	Winter Only	All Year	Summer Only	Winter Only	All Year	Summer Only	Winter Only / All Year	All Year
Impounded	Good	18.964	1.8964	9.482	7.5856	0.75856	3.7928	0.37928	0.037928 / 0.18964	0.009482
Reliant on Storage	Good	9.482	0.9482	4.741	3.7928	0.37928	1.8964	0.18964	0.018964 / 0.09482	0.004741
	Medium	4.741	0.4741	2.3705	1.8964	0.18964	0.9482	0.09482	0.009482 / 0.04741	0.002371
	Poor	2.3705	0.23705	1.18525	0.9482	0.09482	0.4741	0.04741	0.004741 / 0.023705	0.001185
Unsupported	Good	4.741	0.4741	2.3705	1.8964	0.18964	0.9482	0.09482	0.009482 / 0.04741	0.002371
	Medium	2.3705	0.23705	1.18525	0.9482	0.09482	0.4741	0.04741	0.004741 / 0.023705	0.001185
	Poor	1.18525	0.118525	0.592625	0.4741	0.04741	0.23705	0.023705	0.002371 / 0.011853	0.000569

In the Severn/Trent basin also the heaviest charges are on consumption, but the ratio between them and abstraction charges (2.5 to 1) is lower than in the Delaware basin (100 to 1). In France a comparison is more difficult because of the variety of charge rates. Consumption charges average 3.7 ct/m^3 (US ct.0.75/m^3), whereas abstraction charges average 0.1 ct/m^3 (US ct.0.02), or 37 times less. The foregoing particulars can be tabulated as follows:

Table IV.10

SUGGESTED COMPARISON OF CHARGE RATES FOR SURFACE
WATER ABSTRACTION AND CONSUMPTION (1976-1977)

Rates calculated in
US cents per 1000 m^3 per year

Basin	Minimum and maximum rates (rounded)	Range
Severn-Trent	from 0.2 to 7,000	33,333 (including hydropower)
	from 0.9 to 7,000	8,000 (excluding hydropower)
Seine-Normandy	from 6 to 1,500	250
Delaware	from 16 to 1,600	100
Parramatta	from 0.6 to 30	50
Yodo	from 2 to 33	16.5

A leading feature of the surface-water abstraction charge is the large size of the range in rates.

As regards the Yodo and Seine-Normandy basins, in the case of hydropower or water used for power generation reference can be made to installed electric power. Such a comparison yields the following values:

Table IV.11

CHARGES FOR ABSTRACTION AND ELECTRIC POWER
(in 1976 US dollars)

Basin	Rate per MW	Rate per KWh
Yodo	4000	60 ct/KWh
Seine-Normandy	80	1.2 ct/KWh

3. Different rates of charge for different sections of river

This subject has already been mentioned in the preceding paragraph. Along the River Yodo in Japan a tendency is seen towards raising the rates of abstraction charges as one moves further upstream, but these rates of charges reflect various factors in each Prefecture and have no direct relationship with water quality.

In the River Trent basin in the United Kingdom there is no zoning system, but instead a water quality coefficient Q is used. Q = 1 when the water quality is good, Q = 0.5 when average, and Q = 0.25 when poor.

In the Delaware River Basin in the United States all abstraction charges are at the same rate except in the lower estuary zone, where salinity is taken into account, so that here again the rate increases to some extent as the quality of the fresh water improves.

In the Oise and Seine River Basins in France the situation is not so clear-cut, depending on the local situations found along the rivers. The main factor in calculating the rates is the local potential gap between minimum supply at low water and peak demand from agriculture, households and industry. In general, the rates are high where population and industrialisation are dense and there is a risk that supply will fall short of demand. Geographical location (upstream or downstream) and the quality of the untreated water abstracted seem to carry less weight than these quantitative considerations.

The result is that there are clearly defined zones for the different rates of charge which do not coincide with administrative boundaries as in the Yodo basin (where the rates change with the Prefecture), although they do not cut across Commune (municipal) boundaries. The zonal breakdown of the revenue from charges in 1976 shown in Table IV.12 illustrates these points and may be compared with Table IV.5 for the River Yodo.

4. Incentive effect of abstraction charges

The incentive effect of abstraction charges depends on the elasticity of use (elasticity being low for households but high in agriculture), insofar as the elasticity can be ascertained. Consequently, the rates of charge are usually calculated and increased in order to balance the accounts of an investment programme (see Figure IV.1 Seine-Normandy programme) or to redeem loans raised for building storage dams (Delaware). As land use in a river basin becomes more intensive and its water resources are increasingly mobilised, the programmes for making these resources more available tend to expand to offset their growing scarcity. The charges are then raised, but they express only the scarcity of a resource.

Table IV.12

REGIONAL DISTRIBUTION OF REVENUE FROM ABSTRACTION
CHARGES IN SEINE-NORMANDY BASIN (1976)

Oise and Seine River Basins		Revenue from surface water abstraction and consumption charges (in Frs. million)		
UPSTREAM ZONE				
2.0	Upper parts of basins	0.902	0.946	3%
2.1	North Champagne zone	0.002	(M$0.2)	
2.2	South Champagne zone	0.039		
2.3	Reims zone	0.003		
CENTRAL ZONE				
1.1	Greater Paris area, upper	25.664	25.835	92%
1.2	Greater Paris area, lower	0.171	(M$5.2)	
DOWNSTREAM ZONE				
5.0	Lower reaches of the Seine	0.090		5%
3.1	Rouen zone	0.001	1.479	
3.2	Le Havre zone, upper	0.025	(M$0.3)	
3.3	estuary zone	1.363		
TOTAL		28.26m. (US M$5.7)		

MF: millions of francs; M$: millions of US dollars

Abstraction charges may incite users to reduce the wastage of water, especially by industry, and their incentive effect may be considerable in the case of industrial plants (as reported for the Seine and Yodo basins). They may induce thermal power stations and industries which are big users of water to avoid certain zones where abstraction rates are high. However, these users' choices will be guided mainly by quantitative considerations (insufficient guaranteed minimum flow) rather than by economic considerations (too high rates of charge). Abstraction charges are more an economic indicator than an incentive instrument. As a rule they are less effective than pollution charges, but in the case of industry may be set against the marginal cost of water recycling.

5. Level of abstraction charges and inflation

Abstraction charges are adjusted to economic conditions from time to time when programmes for increasing the quantity of water available are revised, but there is no automatic indexation to allow for the erosion of money.

Figure 4.2 gives an idea of the adjustments made for the Seine-Normandy basin.

Figure 4.2

**LEVEL OF ABSTRACTION CHARGES AND
INFLATION (OISE RIVER BASIN)**
*NIVEAU DES REDEVANCES DE PRELEVEMENT
ET INFLATION (BASSIN DE L'OISE)*

Average rate of abstraction charge per m3
Taux moyen par m3 de la redevance prélèvement

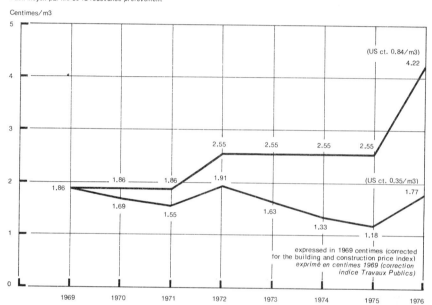

6. Abstraction charges on surface water and ground water

In most cases (the Seine-Normandy and Trent basins are special cases), there is no charge on ground water. In the Yodo basin it is, in most cases, regarded as a free good, while in the Delaware basin and in the other countries covered by this paper it is regarded as a free good.(1)   In the United Kingdom the factor used

───────────

1) In the United States, charges are paid for abstracting ground water in certain areas. In Japan, however, ground water is legally owned by the overlying landowner but, in certain areas where the problem of ground subsidence is serious, abstraction of ground water is strictly controlled.

for ground water in the formula for calculating the charges is standardized (factor 1) and the formula allows for the quality of ground water (three classes: good, average and poor). In the Seine-Normandy basin a rather sophisticated system distinguishes between ground water and surface water, the periods of abstraction, and in certain zones even the types of aquifer.

Abstraction charges on ground water are distinctly higher than on surface water and may be regarded as an economic incentive when surface water can be substituted for less plentiful but better-quality ground water. The aim is to keep ground water for certain (household) uses and prevent it from being wasted on agricultural irrigation or industrial uses which do not require water of good quality.

By way of example the following table gives the 1977 scale of abstraction charges in the Greater Paris Area and the upper basins of the Rivers Oise and Seine (Table IV.13).

7. New abstractors

As a rule the same rates of charge are applied to old and new abstractors, but the latter may have to finance some of the additional water control works (especially storage dams) made necessary by their arrival (this is so in Japan and sometimes in France in the case of large abstractors such as power stations). In addition licence fees may be charged at the time of authorising abstractions (Dommel/Aa and Parramatta basins).

8. Abstraction charges and industrial development

From the examples given in this paper, abstraction charges would not appear to have been introduced as a direct encouragement or discouragement to industrial development. Slight disincentives are applied in river basins whose water resources may impose a constraint on expansion (see the preceding paragraph regarding new abstractors). These charges act much more as incentive instruments under a policy for controlling the wastage of water in terms of quantity and quality (preservation of ground water) than under a policy for siting industries.

Table IV.13

EXAMPLES OF GROUND-WATER ABSTRACTION AND CONSUMPTION CHARGE RATES
IN THE SEINE-NORMANDY BASIN (1977)

Centimes per m³

Zone	Surface water		Ground water	
	from 1.6 to 31.10	from 1.11 to 31.5	from 1.6 to 31.10	from 1.11 to 31.5
Upstream				
Abstraction:	0	0	1.065	1.065
Consumption	3.727	0	3.727 (US ct.0.74/m³) Abstractions from the Albien aquifer	0
Greater Paris area above the Seine-Oise junction				
Abstraction followed by immediate discharge	0.213 (ct.0.042/m³)	0	11.715 (ct.2.34/m³)	11.715
Other abstractions	7.455 (ct.1.49/m³)	1 (ct.0.2/m³)	Abstractions from other aquifers	
Greater Paris area below the Seine-Oise junction	0.032 (ct. $\frac{6.4}{1000}$ /m³)	0	7.455 (ct.1.49/m³)	7.455

Chapter V

ADMINISTRATIVE PROCEDURES

A. IMPLEMENTATION

Administrative procedure varies according to country. Time-honoured custom and conditions specific to each readily account for such differences, while largely disparate features are also found in one and the same country. Cases selected in the present study are therefore in a class by themselves, and cannot always serve as general examples.

1. Enforcement of standards and charges

Relations between responsible authorities and users.

At what level are standards and charges implemented?

The seven case studies agree in distinguishing three levels of authority responsible for water management questions in industrial river basins:

- the country's central or federal government, which enacts outline legislation, lays down procedures and acts, when necessary, as a court of appeal;
- the regional authorities, coinciding with decentralised administrative units (Province, Prefecture, County, etc.) or taking the form of an agency (ad hoc authority or council) specialising in water management (either in a hydrographic basin or otherwise);
- the local authorities, consisting mainly of municipalities, industries and representatives of agriculture. Here the general population or its representatives as a rule are dealt with through advisory committees, associations and public hearings.

The extent to which actions on behalf of water resources management is co-ordinated and the three levels work together smoothly depends on how water management has developed in the past.

The history of water management is usually found at local or regional level and the enactment of laws and regulations at central level is a fairly recent development (dating from the late sixties).

The case studies selected have rather given prominence to the local or regional levels, where management is in the hands of a specialised regional authority (or agency):

- the Severn-Trent Water Authority in the United Kingdom;
- the Dommel and Aa Water Boards in the Netherlands;
- the Seine-Normandy River Basin Financing Agency in France;
- the Delaware River Basin Commission in the United States.

However, the Netherlands is a special case in that the distinction between the central level (Ministry of Transport and Waterways) and the regional level (Water Boards) extends into the field in the separation between "national waters" under the jurisdiction of the Ministry of Transport and Waterways and "regional waters" under the jurisdiction of Regional Water Boards (Waterschappens).

Three countries, Australia, Japan and Sweden, do not have such specifically regional authorities.

In Japan it is the Prefectures (Shiga, Kyoto and Osaka) along the River Yodo which manage water quality, while the quantitative aspects come under the Ministry of Construction. Measures are decreed in agreement with the Central Government (Environment Agency and Ministry of Construction) and in conjunction with a Liaison Committee for controlling pollution of the River Yodo which represents all the levels concerned (including municipalities and industry) and was historically the first body to tackle these questions. The Prefecture, as an executive body, is in an intermediate position between the central legislature and the local advisory body. More specifically, the Ministry of Construction is primarily responsible for such river water management as the licensing of water abstraction and flow control. As to water management in designated river sections as well as some other aspects of management, responsibility is entrusted to Prefecture Governments by the provisions of laws concerned.

In Australia the distinction between central level (Ministry of Planning and Environment) and regional level (Pollution Control Commission of the State of New South Wales) has been blurred since 1974. The regional body has been given responsibility for water management. It comes under a Board of Appeal for Water Resources and has attached to it an Advisory Committee for Water Resources.

In Sweden the three levels exist, but there is a bias in favour of the Central Government level (Ministry of Agriculture with two authorities under it, the National Environment Protection Board and the National Franchise Board of Environmental Protection). Only projects of lesser importance are dealt with directly at regional level (coinciding with the County Administration). At local level the authorities are the Municipal Public Health Committees.

The Delaware River Basin Commission is an exception in the United States organisation. Only one other similar agency exists. Generally the following types of agencies exist in the United States:

- local, metropolitan, regional, multi-county agencies, such as:
  - departments of governments of general jurisdiction, e.g. Department of Public Works of a city or a county;
  - metropolitan water and/or sewerage agencies, such as the Metropolitan Sanitary District of Greater Chicago or of Seattle;
  - special districts, e.g. irrigation districts, reclamation districts, drainage districts, soil conservation districts;
- departments of State governments, e.g. Department of Natural Resources, Department of Environmental Protection;
- agencies of the Federal Government, e.g. EPA, Corps of Engineers.

Who lays down the controls and financial charges?

The regulatory functions (fixing standards) and financial functions (levying charges and distributing aid) are often combined by central or regional authorities. This happens in Japan, the United Kingdom and the United States, and also in Australia, although in the latter country the levying of charges on issuing licences has hardly developed. It does not happen in Sweden, where the regional authorities have none of these financial functions, nor in France, where the Central Government retains the regulatory functions (implemented by the prefectoral services) and some of the financial functions itself, while the river basin financing agencies only have a planning function (they decide what, when and where to build) and a financing function (they collect funds). In this respect the Netherlands is a comparable country.

In the United States, the States have basic responsibilities for water resources management. The Federal Government constructs multipurpose reservoirs and related structures where a "national" interest has been defined, e.g. irrigation, flood damage reduction. With respect to water quality management, the Federal Government approves State-established ambient water quality standards, develops effluent guidelines, approves State-issued or issues discharge permits, subsidises regional water quality management planning, and subsidises the construction of municipal sewerage works by grants and industrial pollution control facilities via special tax depreciation and tax credit provisions. The Federal Government also carries out and finances research, and collects water quality data.

Very often the controls instituted by regional authorities are based on recommendations by the central authorities. Thus the

Delaware River Basin Commission observes the 1972 Amendments to the Federal Water Pollution Control Act of 1948 (PL 92-500); the States apply the National Pollutant Discharge Elimination System (NPDES). However, in the United States the States can set emission standards which are stricter than the Federal guidelines and can, if they choose, levy effluent charges and withdrawal (abstraction) charges. (The states comprising the United States have full power and authority to so act under the United States federal system of government.) In Sweden the policy for preventing pollution follows the 1969 Environment Protection Act and Environment Protection Ordinance, while in the Netherlands the Water Boards are guided by the Pollution of Surface Waters Control Act of 1970.

What activities are undertaken?

The types of activity undertaken by the public authorities differ from one country to another depending on how responsibility for water management is divided among the three central, regional and local levels. As a rule the study and impact evaluation of major water projects come under regional authorities, (although in the United States planning is often carried out at Federal level), whose major functions include the management of low water by means of storage dams, flood and pollution control, hydropower and irrigation. Pollution control is the most recent of these (as for example in the Netherlands), unless authorities have been set up especially to deal with it (as in Australia and France).

Outside the United States, only specific projects are entrusted to local authorities (towns, industries and agriculture). By specific projects are meant those which will little affect the water balance in the basin or river. In the Delaware River Basin the following are regarded as specific projects: impoundments of less than 3.8 million m^3, withdrawals of surface or ground water not exceeding 380 m^3/month (4,500 m^3 per year), secondary waste-water collector systems having a design capacity of less than 190 m^3/day, and changes in land cover affecting less than 780 hectares. Other such projects are for maintaining river beds, temporary construction (bridges and highways), and pipelines designed to operate under pressures of less than 150 psi. For other projects review procedures are required (impact studies submitted to the Basin Commission). Similar provisions have been applied in France since 1st January, 1978.

In what spirit are the controls and charges enforced?

Each case study stresses a reasonable enforcement of standards and charges imposed with regard to the quantity and quality of water used. It is the spirit rather than the letter of the law which should be observed.

Although the law is not leniently applied (particularly in the Netherlands), in practice a conciliatory attitude prevails. Technocratic management procedures are avoided as much as possible. Recourse is had to consultations, enquiries and public hearings. Compliance with abstraction and discharge standards is strictly but not excessively monitored, and the authorities act only in case of consistently serious infringements.

Without discussing public participation in detail (see Chapter VI), an example which should be mentioned is the licensing procedure followed in the Delaware River Basin for polluting discharges (in accordance with the NPDES (National Pollution Discharge Elimination System)

- discussion with municipal, industrial and public representatives of the pollution abatement objectives worked out by the Delaware River Basin Commission;
- public meetings with municipal and industrial officials;
- public hearings at various basin locations to obtain input from local interests;
- Commission staff discussions with concerned companies, cities and individuals;
- presentation by staff at open Commission meetings;
- Commission adoption of allocations;
- informal discussions by Commission staff with industrial and municipal representatives to resolve differences;
- adversary hearings by dischargers objecting to Commission actions before a Hearing Board appointed by the Basin Commission;
- Hearing Board decision;
- court action if deemed necessary by parties involved.

Of 91 allocations, 67 were accepted and in 24 instances hearings were requested. Ultimately eight dischargers withdrew their request for hearings and the 16 others reached amicable settlements without recourse to legal action.

The situation is comparable with regard to licences to abstract water, but one court case should be mentioned to decide a dispute between the Delaware River Basin Commission, the City of Philadelphia and Bucks County regarding payment of abstraction charges by the latter(1).

In France the Seine-Normandy River Basin Financing Agency strictly monitors abstractions and discharges, but a certain laxity in regard to charge payment requirements may be noted. Licences for

1) This situation applying to the Delaware River Basin cannot be regarded as typical throughout the United States.

maximum admissible discharges under the policy for quality objectives are dealt with along much the same lines as indicated for the Delaware River Basin. A "Comité de Patronage" (sponsoring committee) brings together the various interests concerned at public hearings (which are legally oompulsory in the United States). The alternative solutions proposed are considered according to their technical merits, their costs and the individual or local constraints they may involve. Co-ordination between the regional authority (Agence de Bassin) and the central authority is provided by the Mission Déléguée de Bassin, in which the Ministries concerned are represented (Environment, Agriculture, Industry, Supply and Interior). When several administrative regions are involved by a quality objectives project, Comités Techniques de l'Eau Régionaux (regional water engineering committees) act for the Mission Déléguée.

In the Yodo basin, changes in standards and rates of charge are submitted to the Prefectural Assembly for its opinion.

In the Kävlingean basin, public enquiries are made into all major projects.

Compliance with prescribed standards is often strictly enforced (as in the Dommel-Aa basin). Fairly liberal limits are however sometimes applied, as in the Severn-Trent basin, for describing the quality of effluent. In this case it is the frequency of satisfactory measurements which is taken into account in determining whether the polluting discharge is acceptable (see Section V.B below).

In the Parramatta basin, the classification of waters by quality is used more as a reference than for imposing strict control. If measurements of polluting effluents show non-compliance with the licences granted, the Pollution Control Commission sends a notification to the industrialist concerned. It does not usually need to add any warning of legal action in order to obtain compliance, so that here again the aim is to co-operate with the polluters.

2. Have the approved standards really been applied?

Acceptance of the new regulations for protecting the environment is greatly facilitated by the manner described above in which they are applied.

This policy has been assisted by the deliberate simplification of the standards chosen for water protection. Thus only certain quality parameters, usually suspended solids, oxygen content and sometimes toxic substances, have been the subject of specific regulations. More complicated provisions (involving biological indicators and the state of the ecology) are envisaged only for a much later stage. So far micro-pollutants, and pollution which is difficult to measure have been banished, not from the Government's thoughts, but from its dealings with water users, so that it is not surprising that agreement was reached on that part of the problem which is most easily handled namely measurement of abstractions by volume and point discharges of organic and non-organic pollutants.

The charges on the latter have also been accepted. They have not been applied all at once but gradually, so that they might be absorbed smoothly by polluters' budgets. In 1957 the charge in the Netherlands was 0.57 florin per population equivalent per year (US cents 23/pe per year) and had reached 2.75 florins ($1.12) in 1967 and 23 florins ($9.3) ten years later. In France (see Sub-Section III B.12) the increase has been at a similar rate (having quadrupled in seven years).

Only by thus striving for permanent contact among the central, regional, and local authorities can the means available be adapted to the objectives of water protection.

B. MONITORING

There are at least three types of monitoring: a) compliance monitoring of activities using water or affecting water runoff, which monitoring is an integral part of enforcement; b) monitoring of ambient water quality to determine the extent to which water quality standards are being met; and c) biological monitoring of water bodies to determine if achievement of the specified water quality standards does in fact result in the desired aquatic life. (The third type is sometimes considered part of the second type.) The second and third types of monitoring also provide data for the development or improvement of water quality models to enable predicting the effects of changes in discharges on ambient water quality.

In some situations, such as in the Trent River Basin, the agency with overall responsibility for water quality management also operates facilities such as wastewater treatment plants. The monitoring activities of the agency will then include monitoring the performance of its own facilities.

Compliance Monitoring

Monitoring water using and runoff-affecting activities has two components, inspection and measurement. Inspection of the site and operations may be to determine if certain facilities have been installed and are operating, to evaluate "housekeeping procedures", and to check the operation and accuracy of measuring and sampling equipment specified by the licence to withdraw or discharge. Examples of the first for non-point sources include checking whether or not terraces have been constructed and contour ploughing adopted in an agricultural operation, checking whether or not hay bales have been installed at a construction site.

Compliance monitoring is relevant to both point and non-point sources and is directly related to: 1) the type of abstraction controls; 2) the type of discharge controls; and 3) the application of sanctions. The type(s) of abstraction controls and discharge standards - performance, process, product, input - determine what information must be obtained in the monitoring.

Where abstraction and discharge controls are in the form of charges, monitoring is to determine the number of units on which the charge is to be paid. This is true whether the abstraction and discharge are directly to and from a water body, or from a water purveyor and to a communal sewerage facility. If the charges are varied by time of day or time of year, the monitoring has to be designed to obtain the necessary information on time variations in abstractions and discharges.

Where abstraction or discharge controls are expressed as some type of limit, monitoring must be able to determine:

- if a specified flow <u>rate</u> abstracted has been exceeded in relation to one or more specified periods of time, e.g. instantaneous, daily average, weekly average;
- if a specified limit on total quantity abstracted in one or more specified periods of time, e.g. day, week, month, year, has been exceeded;
- if a specified limit on total quantity of a material, e.g. BOD_5, total suspended solids, discharged in one or more specified periods of time, e.g. day, week, month, year, has been exceeded;
- if specified limits on concentration, e.g. mg/l hexavalent chromium, in a wastewater discharge have been exceeded in relation to one or more specified time periods, e.g. instantaneous, daily average, monthly average;
- if the specified limit on a particular constituent in a product, e.g. percentage by weight, has been exceeded;
- if the specified limit on a particular factor input, as a percentage by weight or by total weight, has been exceeded; and
- if the specified performance level, e.g. 85 per cent removal, of a facility, e.g. physical-biological wastewater treatment plant, has been achieved.

Two critical aspects of compliance monitoring merit emphasis. One is the problem of determining the "optimal" frequency and type of sampling to be used, for which determination costs of sampling must be compared with the returns to sampling, in terms of level of compliance. The other is the problem of maintaining quality control over field and laboratory analyses which yield the number on which decisions are based. This is relevant both to the management agency and to the individual water-using activities.

Compliance monitoring provides the basis for enforcement actions, e.g. the application of sanctions. Where abstraction charges and/or effluent charges exist, non-compliance is defined as the failure to apply the charges. Where limits or standards are imposed on abstractions and/or discharges, defining non-compliance is more complicated. Table V.1 indicates some of the relevant questions with respect to defining non-compliance in relation to performance and process discharge standards. Similar questions are relevant to product and input discharge standards and to abstraction limitations.

Having defined non-compliance, the next step is to decide how non-compliance is to be determined operationally, e.g. by required self-measuring and reporting by the abstractor or discharger, by the agency, by some combination. Regardless of whether self-measuring or agency-measuring is adopted, decisions must be made with respect to the following questions:

Table V.1

BASIC QUESTIONS RELATED TO DEFINING NON-COMPLIANCE WITH
PERFORMANCE AND PROCESS DISCHARGE STANDARDS

Is non-compliance defined as the percentage or number of days in a specified time period when average removal is less than some specified level, e.g. percentage BOD_5 removed is less than 85 per cent?

Is non-compliance defined as the percentage or number of days in a specified time period when the specified concentration is exceeded? Exceeded by how much - 10 per cent, 50 per cent, 100 per cent?

Is non-compliance defined as the percentage or number of days in a specified time period when the allowable quantity of discharge, e.g. kilograms of BOD_5 per day, is exceeded? Exceeded by how much?

If limits are specified for more than one residual, how many residuals must be over their limits, and by how much, to be in non-compliance? Does the excess permitted vary among residuals?

Are allowances made for start up/shut down/clean up periods? If so, how are such allowances made, e.g. unlimited variance for a specified time period such as two hours per week? How many times a day, week, year?

Are allowances made for breakdowns and spills? How are accidental spills differentiated from deliberate dumping?

92

Table V.1 (cont'd)

Is non-compliance defined as failure to install some specified equipment or construct terraces or debris basins by a specified date, regardless of the quality and/or quantity of discharge?

Are public facilities - universities, federal/state/local government installations, hospitals, etc. - treated differently for comparable activities than private activities?

What sampling frequency and accuracy of sampling, e.g. accuracy of measuring equipment - flow, sampling analysis - are specified?

What are the costs (capital and O & M) of different types of monitoring equipment for different indicators for different frequencies of sampling and degrees of accuracy?

Is the type of "acceptable" monitoring/sampling equipment specified? Are standards for installation specified?

Who performs the analysis of samples - laboratory of discharger? External laboratory? Is there any system of quality control for laboratory analysis - internal and/or external?

What reporting requirements are specified - content, form, frequency? To which agencies are reports submitted? Are the reports public information? What happens to the reports when filed, e.g. what is the procedure for reviewing and acting on the submissions?

To illustrate, answers to the above questions relevant to the Trent River Basin are presented.

a) The exceedance of any single Consent Condition is a legal contravention of the Consent.

b) Consent Conditions are applicable all the year round; there is no allowance for specific operating conditions.

c) Incidental types of pollution are usually illegal discharges inasmuch as they are "one-off" and hence will not be consented. In such cases any prosecution would be based on the pollution caused rather than the exceedance of Consent Conditions.

d) Non-compliance relates only to effluent quality and not to the non-installation of equipment.

e) Only Crown properties are exempt from legal control but effluents from such establishments invariably comply with desirable standards.

f) The Water Authority analyses all effluent and river samples at its three Regional Laboratories. Quality Control systems are used to check the accuracy of the laboratory data.

g) Effluent data is published by the Water Authority with the agreement of the discharger. A very small minority of

93

dischargers do not allow publication of data. The Control of Pollution Act 1974 when implemented at the end of 1979 will ensure that all effluent data is open to public inspection unless a special exemption certificate is obtained.

Only for the Trent River Basin were data presented on how the management agency defines compliance. For discharges from sewage treatment plants four classes of compliance are defined:

Satisfactory: eight or more out of ten consecutive samples comply with the standards;

Passable: five or less than eight out of ten consecutive samples comply with the standards; and

Unsatisfactory: two or less than five out of ten consecutive samples comply with the standards; and

Very Unsatisfactory: less than two out of ten consecutive samples comply with the standards.

For the year 1976, the compliance record for discharges from publicly owned sewage treatment plants in the Trent River Basin, based on volume, was: satisfactory, 52 per cent; passable, 32 per cent; unsatisfactory, 8 per cent; and very unsatisfactory, 8 per cent. In this particular basin a comparable compilation for discharges from industrial enterprises is not possible, because monitoring is concentrated on discharges which appear to be in violation of licence conditions.

If self-monitoring by the abstractor or discharger is adopted, the role of the management agency then becomes that of inspection to ensure that the specified self-monitoring procedures are carried out accurately. Because the costs and effectiveness of an inspection system are related to the design of the system, some amplification of the problems involved in design, in the form of a set of questions, is merited.

How are the activities to be inspected chosen, e.g. which of the major point and non-point water abstractors and/or dischargers are to be inspected today, this week, this month, this year? Is a random-stratified sample used?

Is frequency of inspection related to size of activity, complexity of activity, past behaviour of activity?

Are inspections performed only when non-compliance is suspected?

What are the costs of inspection with different frequencies of inspection - without and with sampling by inspectors? How do costs vary with the complexity of the operation, e.g. number of points to be sampled, items to be checked?

94

Do inspectors use check lists? Are check lists filed and periodically reviewed to detect chronic violators?

Are inspections unannounced? Held during normal working hours of inspectors or at any time of day? Any day of year? Are "non-inspection periods" explicitly or implicity announced?

What are the qualifications of management agency inspectors? Relative to qualifications of plant personnel, in terms of technological knowledge?

The focus herein is on monitoring discharges, because the information submitted in the case studies indicates that only limited monitoring occurs with respect to water abstractions. However, the principles involved are the same at both "ends". Data with respect to monitoring direct discharges to water bodies in seven river basins are shown in Table V.2.

Three other points can be made with respect to monitoring of discharges, based on the information submitted.

1. The water quality indicators which are sampled, by self-monitoring, the agency, or both, are those which are specified in the licence conditions for the individual discharger. Thus, the indicators measured depend on the character of the activity, and in some cases also on the size. Different indicators would be measured for a food processing plant compared with a metal finishing operation.

2. No information was presented explicitly with respect to the accuracy of measurements required of flow and concentrations of residuals in the flow. In most sewer ordinances in the United States, the accuracy of both flow and of water quality indicators to be achieved by the discharger is specified, e.g. flow accurate to plus or minus 5 per cent, concentration to plus or minus 0.01 mg/1.

3. Monitoring is as relevant for discharges to communal sewage facilities as it is for discharges directly to water bodies. The nature of monitoring required as a function of the system of charges imposed on the discharge to the communal facility: quantity only, or quantity plus quality, where quality may involve several water quality indicators. (See Section III.B for examples of specific charge formulae used.)

Typical charge systems in the United States for industrial discharges into communal systems are based on quantity and at least two water quality indicators, usually BOD_5 or COD and total suspended solids. In a few cases there is also a peak flow charge, or a peak flow limitation. In addition to the charges there may also be exclusions, such as for grease, or limits, such as for pH.

Table V.2

DATA WITH RESPECT TO MONITORING OF DIRECT DISCHARGES
TO WATER BODIES IN SEVEN RIVER BASINS

	Trent (UK)	Parramatta (Australia)	Yodo (Japan)	Kävlingean (Sweden)
SELF-MONITORING REQUIRED	Y[a]	Y	Y	Y
Continuous flow measurement for major discharges required		?	-	Y
Flow estimated		-	-	Y
Frequency of sampling		Specified in Licence	Self-determined	Specified in individual[b] monitoring plan
Type of sampling	Grab	Specified in Licence	Self-determined	Specified in individual monitoring plan
Bioassay or toxicity test required	As required	-	-	Y
MONITORING BY AGENCY	Y	Y	Y	Optional
Continuous flow measurement for major discharges required	Y	?	N	
Flow estimated	-	-	N	
Type of sampling	Grab	Grab	Grab	
Frequency of sampling	Variable	Irregular	Regular	
Depends on size of discharge	Y			
Sampling unannounced	Y	Y	Y	
Bioassay or toxicity test	As required	?	Y	

	Dommel/Aa (Netherlands)	Seine/Nor. (France)	Delaware (US)
SELF-MONITORING REQUIRED	Y	Y	Y
Continuous flow measurement for major discharges required	Y	Y	Y
Flow estimated	-	Y	-
Frequency of sampling	Specified in Licence	Specified in Licence[c]	Daily
Type of sampling	Specified in Licence	24-hour composite	24-hour composite
Bioassay or toxicity test required	As required	Y	As required
MONITORING BY AGENCY	Y	Y[d]	Y
Continuous flow measurement for major discharges required	?	Y	Y
Flow estimated	?	Y	-

Table V.2 (Cont'd)

	Dommel/Aa (Netherlands)	Seine/Nor. (France)	Delaware (US)
Type of sampling	Grab/24-hour composite	24-hour composite	Grab/composite
Frequency of sampling	Random or regular	Irregular	Irregular
Depends on size of discharge	Y	Y	Y
Sampling unannounced	Y	N	Y
Bioassay or toxicity test	As required	Y	As required

a   Includes monitoring of plants operated by river authority.
b   Frequency proposed by discharger, approved by agency.
c   2 or 3 times a year.
d   Agency samples at four locations, upstream and downstream of discharge.

Monitoring Ambient Water Quality

Table V.3 summarises data on the ambient water quality monitoring programmes in the various river basins.

C. ENFORCEMENT

The problem with enforcement relates primarily to achieving compliance with discharge standards. Difficulties in enforcing abstraction standards occur, at least in the United States, primarily during periods of relative water shortage.

Two types of non-compliance with discharge standards can be identified. One is the persistent failure to meet standards, however that may be defined. The other is the deliberate, or accidental, dumping or spilling of effluent into a water body, which may result in sizeable damage to property, aquatic life, other water users.

The procedure for handling non-compliance of the first type seems to be essentially the same in the seven river basins. It involves warnings by, and consultation with, the enforcing authority. The warnings become increasingly stronger until modification of behaviour is achieved, e.g. adherence to standards. If persuasion and reasonable argument are not successful, recourse is to court action, involving either a civil penalty (fine) or jail sentence, or both. Figure V.1 illustrates the court procedure in France. Table V.4 indicates the range of administrative and judicial sanctions available in the United States.

Table V.3

PROGRAMMES FOR AMBIENT WATER QUALITY MONITORING IN SEVEN RIVER BASINS

	Number of Sampling Points	Frequency of Sampling	Water Quality Indicators Analysed
Trent (UK) - Surface Water	182 minor points 351 routine points	Every 3 months Every month	pH, suspended solids, ammonia, total oxidised nitrogen, chloride, BOD (+ATU), dissolved oxygen, temperature, electrical conductivity, total hardness, alkalinity
	62 key points	Every 2 weeks	Above plus total metals, soluble metals, synthetic anionic detergents, BOD (+ATU), TOC, phosphate
	17 special points	Every week	Above plus organochloride pesticides, mercury, boron, arsenic, fluoride, sulphate, non-ionic detergents, iron, manganese
	3 automatic water quality monitors, recording at 15 minute intervals		pH, temperature, dissolved oxygen, electrical conductivity, suspended solids, ammonia
	1 automatic water quality monitor, recording at 15 minute intervals		Above plus organic matter (by ultraviolet absorption) and substances toxic to nitrifying bacteria
	Sampling and analyses are performed by the river basin agency.		

Table V.3 (cont'd)

	Number of Sampling Points	Frequency of Sampling	Water Quality Indicators Analysed
Trent (UK) – Ground water	About 200 wells	Quarterly	Total hardness, calcium hardness, alkalinity, electrical conductivity, pH, BOD, ammonia, nitrate, chloride, sulphate, fluoride, sodium, potassium, iron, manganese, plus cyanide, phenol, other metals where appropriate
	In addition, intensive investigations of ground water quality involving construction of boreholes and subsequent sampling is undertaken where an aquifer is likely to be at risk.		
	Sampling and analyses performed by basin agency.		
Parramatta (Australia)	34 stations	Every 4–5 weeks	pH, dissolved oxygen, salinity, temperature, turbidity, BOD, MBAS, E. coli, nitrogen, phosphorus, chlorophyll a, changes in light penetration and transmissivity, TOC, trace heavy metals
	Sampling and analyses performed by State Government agencies.		
Yodo (Japan)	Unspecified number of sampling points	Once a month	Unspecified
	30 automatic water quality monitoring stations.		Temperature, pH, dissolved oxygen, turbidity, plus electrical conductivity, ORP, cyanide, ammonical nitrogen, COD, TOC, as needed
	Biological sampling	Once every 10 years	
	Sampling and analyses by city, prefecture, and national governments.		

Table V.3 (cont'd)

	Number of Sampling Points	Frequency of Sampling	Water Quality Indicators Analysed
Kävlingean (Sweden)	35 sampling stations	6 times a year	Dissolved oxygen, BOD, phosphorus, nitrogen, bacteria
	Sampling and analyses by water conservancy association.		
Dommel/Aa (Netherlands)	No information available.		
Seine/Normandie (France)	41 points sampled in 1971 and 1976	Once a month or once every 3 months, June through September	Dissolved oxygen, BOD, COD, phosphorus, nitrogen, bacteria, pH, toxics
	Biological analyses	Unspecified	
	Sampling and analyses performed by national agencies.		
Delaware (US)	Number of sampling points on main stream and in estuary unspecified	Twice per month, March through October, once per month November through February	Approximately 30 water quality indicators – mineral, physical, bacteriological – corresponding to those defined in the ambient water quality standards
	Six stations on major tributaries	Once a month at five stations, same frequency as estuary sampling at other stations	
	Several automatic water quality monitoring stations		Electrical conductivity, pH, temperature, dissolved oxygen.
	Sampling and analyses performed by city, state, basin, and national agencies.		

Figure V.1

Punitive Measures Provided Under the French 1964 Act.
Act of 16th December, 1964 (Articles 20 and 21)
Decree of 15th December, 1967 (Article 1)

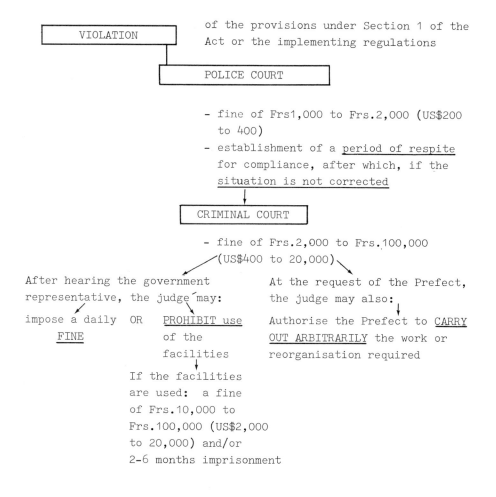

VIOLATION of the provisions under Section 1 of the Act or the implementing regulations

POLICE COURT

- fine of Frs1,000 to Frs.2,000 (US$200 to 400)
- establishment of a period of respite for compliance, after which, if the situation is not corrected

CRIMINAL COURT

- fine of Frs.2,000 to Frs.100,000 (US$400 to 20,000)

After hearing the government representative, the judge may:

impose a daily FINE OR PROHIBIT use of the facilities

If the facilities are used: a fine of Frs.10,000 to Frs.100,000 (US$2,000 to 20,000) and/or 2-6 months imprisonment

At the request of the Prefect, the judge may also:

Authorise the Prefect to CARRY OUT ARBITRARILY the work or reorganisation required

Note: Any person who impedes the monitoring process or the exercise of the functions provided under Article 9 of the 1964 Act (Article 23) shall be liable to 10 days to three months imprisonment and/or a fine of Frs.1,000 to Frs.2,000 (US$200 to 400).

101

The data submitted indicate that in all countries resort to
court action rarely occurs. Substantial fines are levied in some
cases, such as one fine of 10,000 guilders in the Netherlands. Fines
appear to be reserved normally for the second type of non-compliance.
In the United States, where substantial damages have been caused by
spills some court decisions have required the discharger to pay all
damage costs plus large fines.

However, in the context of the continuous management objective
of attaining and maintaining ambient water quality standards, the
crux of the enforcement problem is to induce all dischargers to
meet, within a relatively small margin, their discharge standards
on a day-to-day basis. Otherwise, unless the discharge standards
have been established with a large margin of safety, the ambient
water quality standards will often not be met.

The implementation process is summarised in Figure V.2.

Table V.4

ADMINISTRATIVE AND JUDICIAL SANCTIONS AVAILABLE
IN THE UNITED STATES

ADMINISTRATIVE SANCTIONS BY MANAGEMENT AGENCY(IES)

A. Informal communications

phone calls
site visits
warning letters
   reminder letters
   directive letters
   summoning letters

B. Formal administrative sanctions

administrative orders
consent orders
emergency orders
shut-down orders
sewer bans
civil administrative penalties, e.g. delayed compliance fees
revocation/suspension of permits
permit modification
referral to attorney

C. Ancillary remedies

blacklisting
adverse publicity
withholding of governmental benefits

JUDICIAL SANCTIONS

A. Civil penalties

monetary penalties (fines)

B. Injunctive relief

mandate specific behaviour on part of discharger
prohibit specific behaviour on part of discharger

C. Criminal penalties

fines (usually higher than civil penalties)
imprisonment of corporate or public officials
fines and incarceration

PRELIMINARY FLOW DIAGRAM OF IMPLEMENTATION PROCESS
DIAGRAMME PRELIMINAIRE DES PROCESSUS DE MISE EN OEUVRE

SANCTIONS

COMPLIANCE
CONFORMITE

NON-
COMPLIANCE
*NON-
CONFORMITE*

EVALUATION

Procedural deficiencies - *Départs de procédures*
Permis compliance - *Conformité aux permis*
schedule violations - *Violation d'exécution des plans*
Residual discharge - *Pollution résiduelle*
permit violation - *Violation des permis*

DEFINITION OF
NON-COMPLIANCE
*DEFINITION DE LA
NON-CONFORMITE*

INSPECTION
OF RESIDUALS
MODIFICATION
FACILITIES
*INSPECTION DES
RESIDUS ET
DISPOSITIF DE
TRAITEMENT*

RESULTS OF
INSPECTION
*RESULTATS DE
L'INSPECT.*

REPORTING
RAPPORT

RESULTS
OF S & A
RESULTATS

SAMPLING
AND
ANALYSIS
*ECHANTILLON-
NAGE ET
ANALYSE*

IMPLEMENTATION
INCENTIVES
*INCITATIONS A LA
MISE EN OEUVRE*

RESIDUALS
MODIFICATION
MEASURES
*MESURES DE
MODIFICATIONS
DES RESIDUS*

RESIDUALS
DISCHARGE
*DEVERSEMENT
DES RESIDUS*

PRODUCT
OUTPUTS
PRODUCTION

RESIDUALS
GENERATION
*FORMATION
DES RESIDUS*

ACTIVITIES
Industrial
Agricultural
mining
silvicultural
residential commercial
*ACTIVITES
industrie
ag°culture
mines
sylviculture
ménages commerces*

Data for internal management decisions
Données pour les décisions internes de gestion

INPUTS

AWG

AWG - Ambient water quality
Qualité ambiante de l'eau

103

Chapter VI

USER AND PUBLIC PARTICIPATION

For greater ease of understanding, it will first be well to explain what is meant by "public participation" in the present chapter. Formal participation (defined in laws and regulations) may thus be distinguished from informal, spontaneous participation (depending on public response).

A few instances of participation organised by the authorities are noted below:

- Required formation and use of advisory committees to make inputs in the WQM(1) planning process;
- Required publication and dissemination of WQM plans for comment and discussion at public hearings;
- Required publication (notice) of applications for permits to abstract or discharge, with specified time period for comments and objections;
- Required publication of discharge standards for various industrial and other types of dischargers (as in the United States) with specified time period for comments;
- Permission for private individuals or groups to file court suits with respect to discharge standards, behaviour of specific dischargers, individual permits.

Informal (or spontaneous) participation takes place through debate and discussion in the various media (newspapers, television, radio, etc.). Supporting activities are those of widely varying private interest groups.

Organised formal participation is undoubtedly greatly promoted by the existence of water management agencies at regional or local levels.

Whether formal or informal, public participation in river management decisions (fixing discharge standards, quality objectives and abstractions) is accepted and even encouraged in each of the case studies in this report.

_____

1) Water Quality Management

Such participation has not, however, everywhere been codified by legislation or regulations. Thus, in Australia, Japan and the Netherlands no legislation explicitly provides for participation, although custom and parliamentary tradition are adequate substitutes.

In the other countries public participation is explicitly provided for in the legislation on pollution control: the PL 92-500 Amendments of 1972 and the National Pollutant Discharge Elimination System (NPDES) in the United States; the Loi sur l'Eau (Water Act) of December 1964 and the Loi sur la Protection de la Nature (Nature Protection Act) of July 1976 in France; the Pollution of Surface Waters Control Act of 1970 in the Netherlands; and the Control of Pollution Act of 1974 in the United Kingdom and the Environment Protection Act in Sweden.

As mentioned in Section V.A (Implementation of Administrative Procedures), the approach in taking public opinion into account is a spirit of conciliation and co-operation.

1. Special means used to accommodate the interests of high water quality beneficiaries (potable water and amenity)

In practice the means used by the authorities for making contact with the public affected by water management policy vary with the nature of the contact. The most direct contact consists in discussion between the authorities responsible for making known the rules, standards and charges and the abstractor or discharger concerned. This is the first and most natural step, which is found in all the case studies presented. Another possible method is to broaden the discussion by seeking and evaluating solutions in an assembly consisting of representatives of the public authorities, local users (industry, trade, municipalities and agriculture), residents' interests (nature protection associations and fishing associations) and the government bodies concerned (e.g. the public health authorities). In the Yodo basin each Prefecture has a Prefectural Council for Water Quality which discusses possible solutions, including their technical points and socio-economic impacts. Its conclusions are then submitted to the Prefectural Assembly (or Diet). For the Parramatta, the Parliament of the State of New South Wales plays the same deliberative role. Reports are prepared by the State Commission for Pollution Control which includes members from industry, trade, municipalities and nature protection interests. In France the Agence Financière for the Seine-Normandy basin is controlled by a Comité de Bassin, one third of whose members are representatives appointed by the central government departments, one third respresentatives indirectly elected by the public (from the municipalities), and the remaining third direct water users (industrialists, farmers, fishing associations and local residents). The Comité de Bassin elects the Conseil d'Administration (board of management) of the

Seine-Normandy basin agency from among its members. It notes the latter's five-year action programmes, which state the rates of charge levied and financial aids granted. It reviews the quality objectives of river sections (see below). In the Netherlands the industries and municipalities concerned are represented on the Water Boards.

Still wider public participation, whereby the general public can intervene directly, is provided by meetings and public hearings held when important decisions are to be taken on water management. This is done regularly in the United States, where the discharge standards adopted by the Delaware River Basin Commission are always submitted to the public for their opinion. The industrialists and municipalities affected by these standards submit their briefs to the meetings and account is taken of their objections, approvals, and suggestions. Sometimes those standards which are unsatisfactory as regards river water quality or owing to economic or regional impacts are rejected.

In the Kävlingean basin before a licence is issued, there are public meetings where the polluter and authorities involved are participating; private organisations and persons have the possibility to express their opinion on the polluting activity, the discharge standard and the licence. In the Seine-Normandy basin they are issued in public in pursuance of the policy for quality objectives. A technical report is prepared by the Agence Financière de Bassin jointly with the local authorities comprising:

- information on present water quality and the polluting effluent discharged;
- forecasts of industrial development and population movements; and
- estimates of water requirements for different uses.

This record is forwarded to the Comité Technique de l'Eau (regional administrative level) and then to the Mission Déléguée de Bassin (which includes representatives of the central government). After amendment it is submitted:

- to private and public polluters
- to municipalities
- to the fishing and fish-breeding associations
- to the principal environmental protection associations
- to the local residents' associations
- to the other users' associations (e.g. for tourism and recreation).

Public hearings are then held, some of which are open to all water users. They are political in nature. A confrontation takes place between the demands of the public and the constraints complained of by the polluters. Usually three alternative solutions are discussed:

- the first calls for a minimum of water control works for maintaining minimum quality for certain uses (minimum quality of untreated water as intake for supplying treated potable water);
- the second calls for a timetable for ascertaining the best available technology which is economically practicable;
- the third is more ambitious and aims at satisfying all the calls on a river (including amenity uses).

Once one of the solutions and objectives has been chosen (usually the second, with some modifications), other meetings are arranged, but this time only with the polluters. They are more technical and financial in character and are designed to allocate total admissible pollution between the polluters, having regard to the choice of river quality objectives. The control works required and the possible difficulties are considered case by case.

In the Parramatta basin the classification of rivers by quality ratings is also discussed at public hearings.

- One more type of public participation consists in disseminating information and giving publicity to public enquiries.

In the Delaware River Basin technical and financial information is regularly disseminated and published by the regional and national media (press, radio and television). Forecasts, programmes and future intentions are announced. The correspondence addressed by readers to newspapers show the interest taken by the public in this information and may bring pressure to bear on the attitudes of polluters.

In addition an annual conference is arranged by the Delaware River Basin Commission jointly with the basin's Water Resources Association.

In France the river basin financing agencies issue a quarterly information bulletin and publish the results of their main technical and economic studies. National or local information campaigns are organised with the aid of the media and customary publicity aids (posters, badges, etc.).

In the United Kingdom, under previous legislation, the Water Authority is specifically forbidden to disclose such information to the public without the Consent of the discharger. The Severn-Trent Water Authority do, however, publish annual details of the quality of all its own discharges. Details of the great majority of industrial discharges are also published, although a small minority of industrialists do refuse to give the Water Authority the necessary permission to publish. In these cases the Water Authority publishes a list of the industrialists who have refused to give the Water

Authority such permission. However, the Control of Pollution Act of 1974 will require details of discharges to be publicly available in registers.

The principle of public enquiries also provides an opportunity for wide public involvement, as in the United Kingdom in the case of abstraction licences, which are given publicity in the local and national press. In France steps were taken in 1975 (reform of public enquiries) and 1976 (Nature Protection Act) to undertake a study of the environmental impact of carrying out major projects, the conclusions of which would then be made known to the public.

No particular arrangements for participation seem to have been made for dealing with the specific requirements of potable water supplies and water for amenity purposes. These questions have been the subject of many technical regulations, but are not given separate treatment in public discussions.

2. Procedures for participation by the largest municipalities, industries and industrial plants

It has already been stated that municipalities and industries are almost always represented in the parliamentary assemblies or advisory bodies which discuss problems of water management. Their representatives are usually appointed by decisions of Chambers of Commerce and Industry or of the body superintending the local authorities. At all events, even if there are not explicit participation procedures for this important class of polluter and abstractor, they are in constant touch with the water management authori

3. Level of involvement of polluters, victims of pollution and other water users in the setting of emissions standards and emission charges

This matter was discussed at length under item 1 above, but mention may be made here of the role of certain pressure groups, which may modify the attitudes of the public authorities. These groups are mainly angling associations; in Sweden the salmon and trout fishing association was a particularly active pressure group in protecting water quality in the Kävlingean basin.

Other associations, usually of local residents, can do much good by carrying out studies in depth. This has been noticed in the case of the Dommel and the Aa in the Netherlands, the Water Conservancy Association of Kävlingean in Sweden and the liaison committee for controlling pollution of the Yodo in Japan.

It is difficult, however, to make a quantitative estimate of the influence of such participation on the fixing of standards, objectives and charges, but it may be pointed out that the enforcement of standards and charges is facilitated, if they are well understood and there is prior participation.

4. Does compliance with standards or charges depend on participation?

In some countries the rules governing participation provide for recourse or appeal to a specified body in case the water users concerned are not given satisfaction.

This is so in the Delaware River Basin, but the complaints lodged (see Section V.A.1: Spirit of Enforcement) have been seen to be very few.

In the United Kindgom the law stipulates that the Severn-Trent Water Authority is responsible for any damage caused by dischargers authorised by it, but there has been no case of recourse to the Department of the Environment regarding any of the 900 licences granted. As regards abstraction licences, three appeals to the Department have been made in five years after the issue of 300 such licences.

The small number of law cases seems to indicate a fairly high level of satisfaction.

Conversely the public authorities may sue water users for not paying their charges or not complying with the standards adopted. It would seem that this happens very seldom either in the Netherlands or in France and that a compromise is always sought. Thus for the present the thorny problem of the onus on the water user or public authority to furnish proof does not seem to arise in an acute form.

Generally speaking the experiences described in the case studies would seem to show that the level of involvement of water users varies with the satisfaction they obtain. The more actively they are involved, i.e. the more they concentrate on adopting feasible solutions, the better their interests are served.

The role of economic and social impacts in setting standards and emission charges has still to be studied in view of the lack of quantified experience in that field.

For qualitative objectives the pragmatic solutions would seem to consist in using only the "best practicable means" at the start and in drawing up a quality objectives timetable for rivers.

The most difficult pollution to abate (heavy metals and non-point discharges) should be dealt with later in the light of the technological findings available at the time.(1)

Under these conditions the socio-economic impacts of water management policy should be relatively easy to bear.

---

1) It will, however, be noted that the discharge of certain substances is already absolutely forbidden in the United States, and that quantitative limits are prescribed regarding the use of certain others whose waste products pose cancer hazards.

Chapter VII

REALISATION OF MANAGEMENT OBJECTIVES

PROBLEMS IN ASSESSING ACHIEVEMENT OF OBJECTIVES

A. INTRODUCTION

There are at least five ways in which the objectives of water quality management are expressed. One, perhaps the most common, is in terms of achieving and maintaining specified ambient water quality standards. There may or may not be a time dimension associated with achieving those standards. That is, if present ambient water quality does not meet the specified standards, a given amount of time may be specified in which the ambient standards are to be reached. For example, in the United States, Public Law 92-500 specified that "fishable and swimmable" water quality be achieved in all streams by 1st July, 1983. A second is in terms of the absolute amount of reduction achieved in discharges of various types to water bodies, or the proportion of total generation which is removed. A third is in terms of the proportion of dischargers operating under permits which is meeting the specified discharge standards or the proportion of total discharges which is meeting the specified discharge standards. Fourth, if a programme of capital investments in facilities to improve water quality has been promulgated, to be accomplished over some specified time period such as five years, the extent to which actual investments in facilities coincide with the programme is another measure of the degree of achievement of management objectives. A fifth is in terms of the benefits <u>actually</u> realised from improvements in ambient water quality.

Behind the expression of management objectives in terms of achieving specified ambient water quality standards is a set of assumptions or hypotheses or evidence concerning the benefits which will result if the ambient water quality standards are achieved. These benefits relate to the uses to be made of the given water body, such as for municipal and industrial water supply, irrigation, for water-based recreation, for commercial fisheries. A benefit is also sometimes attributed to the achievement of a desired species diversity in an aquatic ecosystem. Because the relationships between

110

ambient water quality, as measured by various water quality indicators, and the various benefits are not completely defined - especially in monetary terms - one component of assessing achievement is to determine whether or not the reaching of the specified ambient water quality standards does in fact result in the benefits originally hypothesised.

Thus, assessing the achievement of water quality management objectives over time involves measuring: 1) changes in ambient water quality; 2) reductions in discharges to water bodies; 3) congruence with or achievement of a specified programme of investment in water quality management facilities; and 4) benefits attributable to meeting ambient water quality standards.

1. Ambient Water Quality

Ambient water quality is measured by many indicators, such as: dissolved oxygen; pH; chemical oxygen demand; turbidity, as a proxy for suspended solids; total dissolved solids; specific elements such as nitrogen, phosphorus, mercury; algae density; and species diversity. All indicators are not likely to change in the same direction over time, because different types of discharges affect different water quality indicators in different ways. Consequently, over time there may be improvements in some ambient water quality indicators and at the same time deterioration with respect to other indicators. For example, in a number of water bodies in the United States in the last decade, concentrations of organic materials and suspended sediment have decreased, while concentrations of nitrogen and phosphates have increased. Various attempts have been made to develop a single index which combines several water quality indicators to provide some overall measure. The validity of this procedure is not accepted universally.

In order to compare ambient water quality at different points in time, the same water quality indicators should be used. Because of the cost of making measurements of ambient water quality, it is not likely that all relevant water quality indicators can be measured with a frequency and an accuracy sufficient to assess trends. Ideally, to compare ambient water quality at different points in time the measurements should be made under the same stream-flow and air and water temperature conditions. Because of the stochastic nature of these variables, it is unlikely that identical sets of conditions can be achieved at the different points in time. A more operational and more valid procedure is to compare frequency distributions of ambient water quality, based on daily or weekly values over a period of a year, at two or more different points in time, e.g., 5-10 years apart. Of course, all frequency distributions which are to be compared should be based on the same measurement system, or comparable measurement systems, that is, the same frequency of smapling and the same analytical procedures.

However, in assessing the extent to which a water quality management programme has achieved ambient water quality objectives, it is essential to determine if the improvement in or the maintenance of ambient water quality is a direct result of the water quality management efforts of the relevant agency or set of agencies. For example, in a region of declining industrial production, the improvement in ambient water quality which might be observed could be a result of decreased production rather than a result of positive water quality management efforts. Similarly, in an agricultural area in which the mix of crops and management practices changed substantially over time, as a result of changes in factor prices and values of outputs, there could well be an improvement in ambient water quality which had nothing to do directly with the water quality management programme.

Therefore, in order to ascertain whether or not the water quality management programme has produced the improved ambient water quality, there must be a parallel analysis of the trends in the levels of wastewater generating and discharging activities in the region. Indices of changes in levels of activities include population and various measures of physical product output such as tons of steel, number of livestock, barrels of crude throughput, tons of field corn. The levels of activities represent the first rough index of wastewater generation (and water intake). In addition, the changing characteristics of each activity must be ascertained. For example, it is not only the number of people which determines the total quantity of liquid residuals generated by households in an urban area, but also the "life-style" and per capita disposable income. Increasing incomes often result in increased use of water-using appliances, which increases wastewater generation per capita. Similarly, there may be changes in production technology or product mix or product specifications which lead to increased water use and increased wastewater generation per unit of output or per unit of raw product processed. In order to assess the achievement of the water quality management programme, data would be collected on trends in these types of factors as well as data on trends in the levels of discharging activities.

It is important to note that changes in factors not directly related to water quality management, such as changes in enery costs, changes in production technology, changes in product specifications, may result in substantial changes in wastewater generation and discharge. In the United States, following the large increases in energy costs after 1973, a substantial reduction occurred in discharges from a number of industrial operations because of changes induced by the increases in energy costs.

2. Residuals Discharges

Where a water quality management objective is expressed in terms of achieving specified reductions in discharges to water bodies, or in terms of specified degrees of reductions by individual discharges, the degree of achievement of a management programme can be assessed by the extent to which either of these objectives is achieved. The proportion of dischargers meeting standards can be determined, assuming that the term "meeting the standards" has been defined, given the stochastic nature of discharges. However, the percentage of dischargers meeting the standards is not likely to be a very good measure of achievement, because it is not necessarily a good index to the total quantity of reductions in discharges achieved. Often a relatively small number of large dischargers in a region discharge a large proportion of the total discharged in the region. If all of these are in compliance or have achieved their discharge standards, then most of the reductions in discharges targeted may have been achieved, although a relatively small proportion of the total number of dischargers is in compliance. Conversely, a large proportion of the total number of dischargers may be in compliance, but if a few large dischargers are not, then the total discharge of residuals to water bodies may be substantially higher than the targeted magnitude. A better index of the extent to which a management programme is achieving its objectives would be the proportion of residuals generated which are not discharged. However, even this index can be misleading if the quantity generated is growing substantially with the growth of the individual activity category. Thus, even if the proportion generated in a region which were not discharged increased, if total generation increased as much or more, then there would be no reduction in discharge, even though the water quality management programme had had positive impacts on individual dischargers.

As with various indicators of ambient water quality, so with residuals discharges. The trend in discharge of some residuals may be decreasing, whereas the trend for other residuals may be increasing. For example, in some agricultural areas in the United States, the trend in discharge of suspended sediment has shown a decline, because of the effects of conservation measures, whereas the trends in discharges of nitrates and phosphates have shown significant increases.

3. Water Quality Management Expenditures

Where a programme of public investment in water quality management facilities has been adopted, for example for a five year period, the degree of achievement in accord with that programme can be readily assessed in terms of the actual pattern of expenditures. However, expenditures in terms of investment do not necessarily have any direct relationships to improvement in ambient water quality. Facilities can be constructed but inadequately operated. Often the facilities may be financed by one level of government, leaving the day-to-day operation and maintenance expenses to be financed at another level of government having inadequate resources to allocate to those expenses.

To achieve improvement in or to maintain ambient water quality requires expenditures - for capital investment, operation and maintenance, and administrative costs for planning, monitoring, inspecting, licensing - by both public and private entities. Some of these water quality management costs are straightforward, such as the construction and operation of a sewage treatment plant by a municipality, river authority, or industrial operation. Other costs are more difficult to identify, because they may be in part modifications of production processes stimulated for reasons other than reducing discharges, or because they may result in the recovery of some used material or energy or in byproduct production, such that the net cost of reducing discharges is decreased. An agricultural operation may shift to minimum tillage in order to reduce soil loss, but such a shift may simultaneously reduce the amount of energy used per ton of crop output. The shift may also lead to increased herbicide use and hence to an increase in discharge of herbicides into water bodies. The shift to minimum tillage may also help to maintain the long-run productivity of the soil, so that the shift may be stimulated by that objective rather than a water quality management objective. The addition of a centrifuge to the "white water" system of a paper mill will result in reducing suspended sediment discharge, but will also increase fibre recovery and hence reduce raw material purchases. These are just a few of the many examples in which there are joint cost-joint product problems which make it difficult to identify what legitimately can be attributed to water quality management costs in the private sector.

Finally, the difficulty of determining water quality management costs in the private sector is further exacerbated by the fact that factors unrelated to water quality management may have indirect impacts on discharging activities. Increased cost of pulp wood may lead to an increased use of waste paper as a raw material, which in turn will change significantly the quantity of wastewater generated.

4. Benefits

Even where relatively definitive relationships between discharges of residuals to water bodies and the resulting ambient water quality can be defined, there remains the problem of relating the resulting time and spatial pattern of ambient water quality to benefits. Because benefits are directly related to the uses individuals and various activities make of water bodies, the problem of benefits is directly related to the perceptions individuals have of ambient water quality. What appears to be high quality water to one individual may appear to be low quality water to another individual. Use patterns, and hence benefits, are significantly affected by perceptions.

To conclude, no simple, single measurement suffices for assessing the results of some water policy or system of management. The few examples which follow show how complex the subject is, by making use of the four criteria defined above.

B. EXAMPLES OF RESULTS

1. Changes in Quality of Surface Water

All the countries which contributed to this report have succeeded in improving their water quality.

In the River Kävlingean in Sweden, for example, $BOD7$ fell from over 7mg/l in 1968 to under 3.5mg/l in 1976 and phosphorus in terms of phosphate fell from over 500microg./l to under 200microg./l.

Another yardstick for measuring the improvement in water quality is the concentration of dissolved oxygen. In the River Parramatta in Australia the concentration is approaching saturation, as shown in Figure 7.1.

A still more realistic way of assessing the progress achieved is to show the dissolved oxygen profile of a river which has suffered serious pollution. Data collected for the Delaware estuary shows that the lowest point on the profile was increased between 1967 and 1976 (from 1 to 2mg/l) and that the section of river which does not comply with the prescribed quality standard has become shorter (about 30 miles instead of 65 miles), although it has not yet disappeared.

A very long series (starting in 1900) recorded for the River Yodo in the area of Osaka in Japan shows: a gradually increasing trend of COD (in terms of potassium permanganate) from 1900 to about 1950; a rapid increase after the Second World War to about 1970; and a sharp decline since. The decrease is a result of the water treatment policy followed since the middle 1960's.

Instead of merely taking the variation of a single parameter, a more general idea can be obtained of the improvement in water quality by considering several criteria of organic pollution as given, for example, in the following table (the Katsura is a tributary of the Yodo).

Figure 7.1

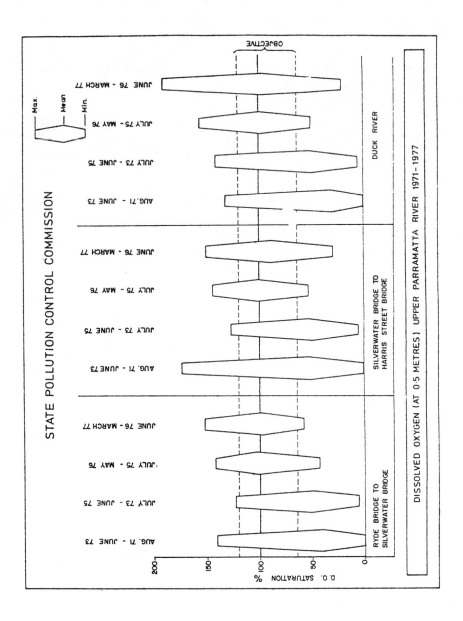

Figure 7.2

Trend of Ambient Water Quality in terms of
Chemical Oxygen Demand, right bank of Yodo
River at Kunishima.

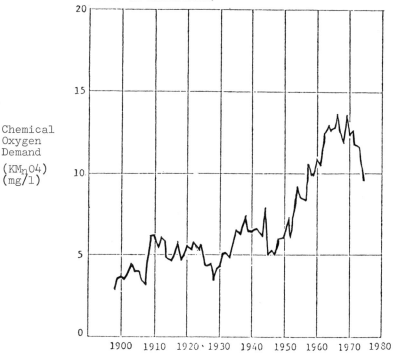

Table VII.1

WATER QUALITY AT MIYAMAE BRIDGE IN THE KATSURA RIVER (JAPAN)

(yearly average value)

Item	1966	1967	1968	1969	1970	1971	1972	1973	1974	1975
pH	7.0	7.1	7.1	7.0	7.2	7.3	7.2	7.3	7.2	7.1
BOD mg/l	11.8	14.8	16.0	23.4	12.5	13.3	10.8	12.7	16.1	8.4
COD mg/l	8.1	7.9	11.1	10.8	8.9	-	-	16.1	17.0	10.3
SS mg/l	-	-	-	30.8	34.1	27.0	25.7	39.6	51.2	17.4
DO mg/l	5.3	5.2	4.9	4.8	9.3	5.9	6.4	5.8	7.0	8.1
Number of coliform groups (MPN/100ml)	9.5×10^5	7.4×10^5	7.7×10^5	1.1×10^6	5.2×10^5	2.2×10^5	5.3×10^5	2.2×10^6	1.7×10^6	2.6×10^5

118

Comparisons can then be made with the targets which had been set.

Table VII.2

CHANGES IN POLLUTION LOADING AMOUNT IN THE YODO RIVER

(BOD ton/day)

Water Body	Year	1970 (Achievement)	1976 (Goal)	1975 (Achievement)
Katsura River (The upper stream from Miyamae Bridge)		64.84[1]	37.95[1]	55.34[2]

1) Environmental pollution control programme of the Yodo River Basin in Kyoto Prefecture.
2) Reported by Osaka and Kyoto Prefectures.
   The values for the 1976 (Goal) column, are the values of the provisional goal to be achieved in the course of attaining the final goal.

This leads to the cencept of rating each section of river according to a quality class, as shown in the following extract from a table drawn up for the River Trend. (The quality classes are those recommended by the Commission of the European Communities, and are shown in Table II.3).

Table VII.3

CHANGES IN RIVER QUALITY IN TRENT BASIN - (1953-1976)
ANNUAL AVERAGE RIVER QUALITY DATA

River	Sampling Point	Date	BOD (mg/l)	NH_3 (mg/l)	River Classification	Comments
Dove	Trent confluence	1953	5	0.2	2	High quality river used as a drinking water source.
		1962-64	4	0.4	2	
		1971-73	2.7	0.2	1	
		1975-76	1.7	0.1	1	
Derwent	Trent confluence	1953	9	0.9	3	Transformed from a fishless river in 1953 to a public water supply. Now supports a thriving fishery.
		1963-64	4	0.9	2	
		1971-73	4	0.6	2	
		1975-76	4	0.6	2	
Soar	Trent confluence	1953	14	3.6	3	Precarious fishery now restored to a good fishery despite substantial increase in effluent content.
		1962-64	7	7.8	3	
		1971-73	7	4.0	2	
		1975-76	6	0.8	2	

Changes in river quality may not be homogeneous for all polluting parameters taken into account. Table VII.4 shows the relative
weights in 1971 and 1976 of parameters characterizing water quality
in the Seine-Normandy Basin. In 1971 the parameters BOD_5 and oxidisable matter was still as significant but ammonium had increased
significantly in relative importance.

Table VII.4

FREQUENCY OF RESPONSIBILITY FOR
WATER DEGRADATION IN THE SEINE-NORMANDY BASIN

Main parameters responsible for degradation	Quality 3 class (Mediocre to poor water quality)		Quality 2 class (Average water quality)	
	1971	1976	1971	1976
COD	34%	21%	11%	13%
BOD_5	27%	22%	30%	21%
Ammonium NH_4^+	26%	32%	10%	21%
Fecal streptococci	19%	20%	26%	23%
E. Coli	0	0	51%	48%
Anionic detergents	12%	2%	8%	1%

(Column totals may exceed 100%, as certain streams may be mainly
  degraded by more than one polluting factor).

While the foregoing results show that some knowledge of changes
to the natural environment is available, the fact remains that often
too few data over too short a period are available to be able to
assess trends accurately.

While the information collected by all the countries which
contributed to this report is fairly adequate as regards organic
pollution (DO, COD and BOD) and suspended solids (SS), it is not so
as regards toxic substances, heavy metals, micro-pollutants, and
bacterial and viral pollution. To a lesser extent the information
on phosphorus and nitrogen in river water is still fragmentary.
Here lies one of the major difficulties in furthering pollution
knowledge, namely how to assess the impacts of non-point discharges
and uncover changes in the factors degrading the water quality of a
stream soon enough.

2. <u>Quantitative trend of abstractions and polluting discharges</u>

The measuring methods (metering for abstractions and standards
and charges for discharges) adopted in recent years have made water
users more careful in their uses of water. Indirectly they have also
provided a valuable source of statistical information.

Table VII.5 and Figure 7.3, worked out for the Seine-Normandy Basin in France, show the effect on industrial demand of levying charges on quantities of water abstracted (an effect not felt by household abstractors).

Figure 7.3

TREND OF ABSTRACTIONS
Water from all sources - Millions of m3 recorded
EVOLUTION DES PRELEVEMENTS
Eau de toutes origines - Millions de m3 relevés

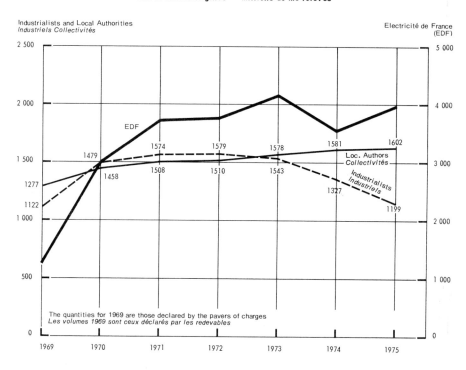

Table VII.5

TREND OF ABSTRACTIONS, SEINE-NORMANDY BASIN

Period 1969-1975

WATER FROM ALL SOURCES

m³ thousand

	1969	1970	1971	1972	1973	1974	1975
Abstractions by local authorities	1,277,940	1,457,860	1,507,980	1,510,640	1,578,301	1,590,971	1,601,651
Abstractions by industry	1,122,040	1,479,580	1,574,310	1,579,290	1,542,980	1,326,791	1,198,783
Abstractions by Electricité de France	1,247,680	2,931,740	3.702,460	3,769,540	4,158,030	3,664,945	3,959,048
TOTAL Seine-Normandy Basin Financing Agency	3,647,660	5,869,180	6,784,750	6,859,470	7,279,320	6,582,707	6,759,482

122

In the Yodo River basin, the demand for water along its lower reaches shows an annual increase of 1.6 percent for household use and an annual decrease of 6 percent (from 1972 to 1976) for industrial use, giving a very slight increase (+ 0.3 percent per year) in total quantities abstracted. These trends, however, are regarded as the consequence of slow-down in economic activities particularly since 1973, and not as the effect of levying charges.

Table VII.6

WATER ABSTRACTIONS IN THE YODO BASIN BELOW THE
CONFLUENCE OF THREE RIVERS

	City Water	Industrial Water	Total
1970	1,296	0,577	1,873
1971	1,346	0,619	1,965
1972	1,424	0,620	2,044
1973	1,415	0,587	2,002
1974	1,382	0,535	1,917
1975	1,424	0,499	1,923
1976	1,426	0,481	1,907

In North Brabant Province, the Netherlands, a similar process is noted.

Figure 7.4

GROUND WATER ABSTRACTIONS IN
NORTH BRABANT PROVINCE

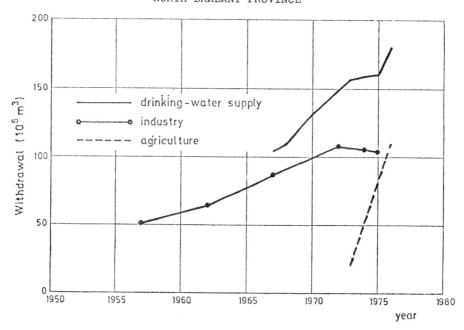

b) <u>Reduction of polluting discharges</u>

The changes in polutting discharges are often not so well known. Information on them is easier to obtain by levying charges on discharges. For example, it is estimated that in the Seine River Basin in France the percentage of pollutants generated, which were removed, varied from 75 percent in 1969 to 54 percent in 1973. The one water management target is to lower this figure to 39 percent by 1982 and to 20 percent by 2000. This plan makes it possible to chart the course of pollution as a whole (reckoned in terms of suspended solids and oxidisable matter only), as shown in Figure 7.5.

Figure 7.5

LONG-TERM TREND OF POLLUTION IN THE BASIN
(SEINE-NORMANDY)
EVOLUTION A LONG TERME DE LA POLLUTION DU BASSIN
(SEINE-NORMANDIE)

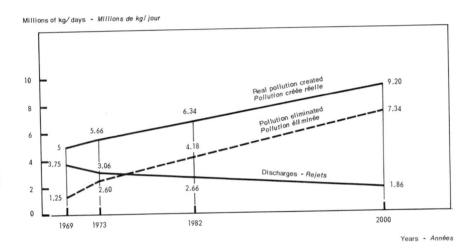

In the Delaware River Basin in the United States a similar quantification makes it possible to calculate what has been achieved from the overall amount of pollution admissible for discharge into the river, as shown in Table VII.7.

Table VII.7

NUMBER OF DISCHARGES CONFORMING WITH FIXED QUALITY
OBJECTIVES IN THE DELAWARE RIVER BASIN

	Number of conforming municipal discharges	Number of conforming industrial discharges	Degree of success, or cumulative proportion of waste load admissible for discharge into the river
May 1974	14	15	7%
April 1975	+ 15	+ 16	11%
During 1977		+ 16	24%
Planned for the 1980s	+ 28	+ 14	60%
Town of Camden, New Jersey, Philadelphia	+ 2		100%

In the Trent Basin measurements have shown an improvement in
the overall composition of urban effluents, whose volume increased
by 12 per cent between 1973 and 1976, whereas their waste load in
terms of BOD decreased by 3 per cent, so that the average waste load
discharged per unit of volume decreased by 13.5 per cent during the
period.

The Dommel-Aa Basin shows considerable improvement in relation
to discharges of heavy metals.

Table VII.8

HEAVY METAL DISCHARGES BY INDUSTRY
IN THE DOMMEL-AA BASIN

	1973	1974	1976
	(ton)		
Aa	30	25	13
Dommel	158	78	52

3. Programme Achievement

The assessment made of the impacts of the integrated management
of water resources which has been tried for some years now is in
line with the preceding numerical data.

Generally speaking, the increase in pollution has been halted
and in many cases there are even clear signs of improvement, so that

the efforts being made are at least capable of arresting the natural increase in pollution due to urban and industrial growth. Sometimes they even make up the lag in pollution control.

The real difficulties are due to shifting aspects of the problem, such as the replacement of point discharges by non-point discharges (Delaware, Seine-Normandy Basin, Parramatta, Trent and Kävlingean River Basins) and to the increased virulence of certain factors, such as mitrogenous substances and phosphorous (Trent, Seine-Normandy, Yodo and Parramatta Basins) and toxic substances (Delware and Seine-Normandy Basins). Results have already been achieved, however, as in regard to toxic substances in the Yodo Basin and Lake Biwa, where a special abatement programme has been carried out (notably for cadmium and mercury, minimum standards for which were first achieved and then bettered). Special efforts are likewise being made to abate artificial eutrophication. In the Delaware Basin a reduction in ammoniacal nitrogen has been recorded, although fecal coliforms, water temperature and phosphate content continue to increase. In Sweden the Kävlingean Basin's phosphorous content has slightly diminished in recent years. In the case of the Dommel, the programme has succeeded in obtaining a quality better than or equal to category three in all sections, a result which took ten years to achieve and will be bettered in the next few years.

It should be noted, however, that these finishing touches are increasingly costly and come up against financial constraints.

As regards quantities of water abstracted, a close qualitative connection should be noted between policies for preventing waste of water and policies for protecting the environment. While the demand for potable water for communities and irrigation water for agriculture keeps increasing and industrial requirements are tending to decrease, river training (maintaining a minimum flow and lowering peak flood levels) is still one of the main problems governing economic development in river basins with too little water (the Oise Basin in France, the Yodo Basin in Japan and the Trent Basin in the United Kingdom).

From the standpoint of administrative results, the following tendencies appear to prevail.

New legislation decided on in the late sixties or early seventies for controlling pollution was introduced and enforced without any particular difficulty and with the broad approval of water users concerned.

Minimum standards laid down by central authorities have often been tightened by local authorities (as in the Yodo Basin).

The levying of charges where they exist (Seine-Normandy and Dommel-Aa Basins), has been well received and the revenue from them has grown steadily (while the assessment basis has diminished), as is well illustrated in the Seine-Normandy Basin in France.

Figure 7.6

TREND IN REVENUE FROM CHARGES IN THE SEINE-NORMANDY BASIN

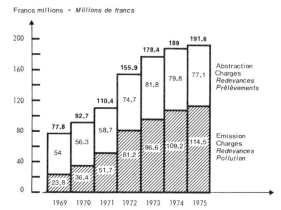

TOTAL CHARGES LEVIED
ENSEMBLE DES REDEVANCES EMISES *

Francs millions - *Millions de francs*

* Seine-Normandy Basin
  Bassin Seine-Normandie

The sum of efforts carried out is shown by the following tables
and figures:

Table VII.9

ACCOUNT FOR 1969-1975. AID PAYMENTS GRANTED FOR POLLUTION CONTROL

Francs million

Conventional pollution (SS and OM)	Number of projects	Cost of works decided on	AID PAYMENTS			
			Subsidies	Loans	Advances	Total
Disposal and treatment works						
- Municipalities and connected industries	1,115	1,498	418.2	64.7	71.8	554.7
- Industries with own facilities	528	376.4	67.5	81.5	35.6	184.6
Saline pollution	2	35.3	10.2	13.8	-	24
Toxic pollution	93	94.8	25.8	29.9	0.1	55.8
Other projects (semi-liquid and solid wastes, technical assistance, measurements, maintenance and operation of waste treatment stations)	503	112.8	35	21.5	-	56.5
TOTAL	2,241	2,117.3	556.7	211.4	107.5	875.6

127

Table VII.10

INVESTMENT PROGRAMMES

a) River Dommel Water Board

Period	Investment (10^6 Dfl)	Cumulative Investment (10^6 Dfl)
1951-55	0.7	0.7
1956-60	4.3	4.9
1961-65	17.3	22.2
1966-70	10.5	32.7
1971-75	133.5	166.1
1976-78 (3 years)	64.3	230.4

b) River Aa Water Board

1963-67	4.8	4.8
1968-72	29.3	34.1
1973-77	50.8	84.9
1978-79 (2 years)	8.5	93.4

Figure 7.7

TREND OF COMMITMENTS OF THE AGENCY FROM 1969 TO 1975 *
(in millions of francs)
EVOLUTION DES ENGAGEMENTS DE L'AGENCE DE 1969 A 1975
(en millions de francs)

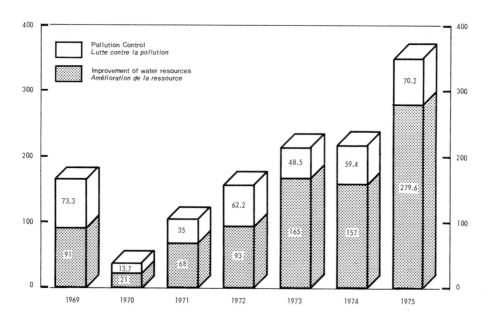

* Seine-Normandie

128

4. Benefits obtained by improving the receptor medium

This is a difficult question owing to the lack of numerical data, especially as regards benefits yielded by a water management policy in monetary terms. Some tendencies may however be suggested without purporting to be a proper appraisal of the policies pursued.

Each case study tries to show the importance of preserving the environment from the effects of pollution, but it is difficult to put a value on improved living conditions. The protection of oyster-breeding and fish-breeding grounds is one possible approach (Delaware Basin), but is only partial. The same applies to the effects of a water management policy on the possible amenity uses of water.

A wider approach, still only at the experimental stage, is to employ matrices of water uses grouped in quality classes (IA, IB, 2, 3 and 4) used in the Trent and Seine-Normandy Basins for describing the quality of river water. For example, classification of a section of river in category IB would mean that intake pipes could be inserted for obtaining potable water after low-cost treatment.

The benefits derived from a water management policy which increases the quantities of water resources are easier to evaluate. They are seen in the urban and industrial development which then becomes possible and is in itself an indicator of what is at stake in water management. In this respect the River Yodo belongs to the group of five pilot projects developed in Japan for the quantitative improvement of water resources. The scheme to control the level of Lake Biwa should soon add 40 m3/s to the flow available.

Flood control (on the Delaware, Yodo and Parramatta) is also a benefit relatively easy to quantify, so that the control works (dams, straightening of river beds, etc.) carried out have a counterpart which can be evaluated.

The other economic impacts (especially on employment) of policies for managing industrial river basins have not so far been studied very thoroughly, but some attempts to modelise water management, which are discussed briefly in Chapter VIII below, try to give a rough idea of them.

Chapter VIII

WATER MANAGEMENT POLICY AT RIVER BASIN LEVEL

The following are the main points made in the various case
studies on which this report is based:
- There are several typical stages in introducing a water
  management policy in an industrial river basin.
- There is a tendency towards integrated management of surface
  waters and ground waters, as regards both quantity and
  quality, covering the technical, financial and administrative
  aspects.
- While complying with the existing legislation, a consensus is
  sought when disputes arise between waters users and water
  management authorities.
- Is quality compatible with economic development? Sooner or
  later this question arises when the technical and financial
  resources are limited.

1. Competition between uses; establishment of hierarchy and
    priorities

Generally speaking, the development of competition between different uses is limited by administrative controls which endeavour
to treat all water users as fairly as possible by fixing standards
or applying financial measures on a non-discriminatory basis.

Nevertheless in critical periods (e.g. a drought, when abstractions of water have to be rationed) conflicts may arise and the need
will then be felt to fix priorities for different uses. This happened in Japan in 1973 and 1977, when restrictions had to be established by a conference on drought attended by water users and the
authorities.

Preferred treatment was given to household users of water
(potable water supplies). During a first stage licensed abstractions were reduced by 10 per cent for towns and 15 per cent for
industries, and during a second stage in 1973, these reductions
were stepped up to 20 per cent and 25 per cent respectively. Agricultural abstractions, which peaked at 4 m3/s, were not changed.

Here, mention should be made of the part played by the Liaison Committee of the River Yodo municipal and industrial water users and by the Liaison Committee for controlling pollution of the River Yodo.

Similar behaviour could be observed during the drought in France in 1976.

The Comités de Patronage (sponsoring committees) set up for rivers when the policies for surface water quality objectives were introduced make it easier to understand the measures taken, which may favour certain water users by ranking abstractions or discharges in order of priority.

Other possible conflicts concern the balance to be preserved between upstream and downstream water users in a river basin.

In Sweden, for example, the Malmö-Lund district abstracts a considerable amount of water from Lake Vorbsjön, which is of critical importance at low water periods owing to the flow of the River Kävlingean which it feeds.

There are similar conflicts in Japan regarding the rules for regulating the Yodo. People living on Lake Biwa (especially fishermen and farmers) object to the use of the lake's water during a drought for supplying the needs of the Kyoto-Osaka urban and industrial concentration downstream. Releases from the storage dam on the Seta (a tributary of the Yodo) are made in a spirit of neutrality and solidarity by the Bureau of Construction for the Kinki area which comes under the Ministry of Construction.

Similarly in the United States the withdrawals by New York City from the upper Delaware are subject to preserving a minimum flow in that river.

2. Implementation strategies and the resolution of conflicts which may arise

As already stated, the participation by interests concerned in decision making must be allowed for by means of administrative procedures and mechanisms so that any conflicts which arise between water users and the authorities can be prevented or best resolved.

The method generally adopted is to set up water users' committees, but attention should be drawn to the administrative difficulties which may arise if committees, riverside residents' associations, and defence and nature protection movements proliferate. This has happened in the Delaware Basin where the Basin Commission has an increasingly difficult co-ordinating role to play because of the number of negotiating parties acting through representative groups.

Thus, a balance has to be found between representation of interests at ground level (through river committees) and liaison between water management authorities and regional and national political assemblies. It is for the latter to choose democratically among policies proposed for developing the river basin after weighing up their socio-economic impacts. This is the strategy followed in France, the Netherlands and the United Kingdom.

Apart from the conflicts which may arise between water users there are also others which should not be overlooked or underestimated. These are conflicts between certain water users and the authorities, and those implicitly arising between generations whenever the financial cost of long-term programmes is apportioned.

The construction of storage dams or wastewater treatment plants is a good example of the first type of difficulty (between water users and the authorities). More and more often the siting of storage dams or protected zones (e.g. boundaries of protected catchment areas) encounters opposition from local farming interests and disapproval by ecology movements of the conservationist type which wish to curb as much as possible any schemes involving alterations to existing ecological balances.

Likewise the disamenities experienced near treatment plants (landscape, odours and social attitudes) are flatly opposed by the urban water users concerned.

These two types of example, which may be observed in France and the United Kingdom, illustrate the ambiguous situation of the authorities, urged on the one hand by public opinion to carry out plans for improving the natural environment, but held back on the other hand from giving them practical effect in the form of the necessary installations.

The solution generally adopted for resolving these contradictions is to consult users' committees which stand above the level of local conflict and to seek a decision from regional and national political assemblies.

The conflicts between generations are less conspicuous. The point is that the responsible authorities must always be careful not to place financial burdens on future generations and leave them to solve problems inadequately dealt with today. In this regard, the adapting of financial resources to the requirements of a long-term water management policy is certainly the most effective course.

One further type of conflict to be resolved is between or among administrative organisations themselves. The most striking example is between States which border on the same river or share the same river basin (in the case of the Delaware four different States are involved). Rather than resort to Federal or national arbitration of conflicts, which would be cumbersome and hinder dynamic management of the basin, it would seem more suitable to deal with such difficulties by setting up a co-ordinating body for the regions or States concerned. The Delaware River Basin Commission and the Agences Financières de Bassin in France have clearly shown how effective they can be in this capacity.

3. Water policy planning (water management and quality) and the scope for development (regional and industrial)

The Pollution Control Commission for the State of New South Wales recently published a report on the relationship between the quality of watercourses and growth in the Sydney area. The main points made in it clearly state the problem:

- What types of activity degrade the quality of watercourses?
- What are the amounts and physico-chemical characteristics of discharges in dry weather and in flood conditions?
- How are polluted effluents collected, treated and discharged?
- What technical and economic constraints are involved in the latter operations?
- What conclusions are to be drawn from a comparison between the growth of disposal and treatment facilities and the demographic and economic growth of the region?
- What are the effects of urban and industrial growth on sensitive sections of rivers and estuaries?

In order to answer these questions, i.e. to try to reconcile the quest for better water quality with continued regional development, it is usually necessary to decide on objectives for water policy and make plans for achieving them.

The objectives adopted in the Netherlands are to restore the ecological function of watercourses (to stop disturbing the aquatic ecosystem) and enable specific requirements to be met (supplies for treatment to provide potable water and for recreational uses). In the United States, the nature of objectives has changed with time. During the 60s, the prime objective was to increase the quantity of dissolved oxygen in rivers mainly by reducing the BOD of pollutants from point sources. This objective, which would promote fish life and various water uses, was to be achieved by constructing municipal and industrial waste treatment plants and making certain technological changes in industries. During the 70s the problem of regional growth emerged as an obstacle to achieving these objectives. The extent of pollution from non-point sources sometimes proved to be about as great as that of modified discharges from point sources. Pollution increased in complexity and in addition to organic pollution there were toxic substances, micro-pollutants and carcinogens which gave cause for alarm. There was then a shift in objectives. The country's requirements were no longer limited to fishing and bathing, but called for protection of the integrity of the aquatic ecosystem, a much more ambitious goal. Concern for the protection of public health, supply of potable water and achievement of the foregoing goal has now given rise to controversy. The question is whether it is more costly to solve the problems of water pollution by technological means irrespective of the interests of regional development, or whether it is preferable to control the introduction of new activities by so planning land use as to prevent further urban and industrial concentration. The latter option would mean explicit competition between uses of public resources (in this case the natural environment and water). In practice, the two alternatives are not independent of each other, and the solution is to mix both approaches.

In Sweden the objectives of water management policy are to maintain or achieve a river water quality good enough for providing potable water after limited treatment and without hindering the free exercise of leisure activities.

In France, the objectives were thought out when long-term plans and the policy for river quality objectives were drawn up. Between 1969 and 1975 thirty-year plans published in the form of river basin white books set forth a policy for an initial clean-up. The aim was to reduce the BOD of rivers by 80 per cent by the end of the century so as to bring pollution down far enough for waste assimilative capacity to complete the job. This meant arresting pollution at its 1975 level and then bringing down organic pollution. During a second stage (1977-81) the aim is to achieve a minimum dissolved-oxygen content in rivers. Studies are conducted by separate river sections, and require determination of the most restrictive parameter for obtaining a certain amount of dissolved oxygen. After BOD, ammonium content or the presence of micro-pollutants is often a constraint which must be overcome.

As in the United States, the concept of pollution has hence broadened and diversified in recent years. Matrices of desired uses for sections of rivers are shown to the local population so that, in the light of their choices, the maximum levels of polluting discharges, including several admissible pollution parameters, may be determined. This procedure for establishing river quality objectives has been followed in the Oise River Basin since 1973.

Under this procedure three kinds of difficulties have to be solved:

- technical: . establishing desired uses for the water
. determining what quality of water is suitable for these uses
. maximum values of critical polluting parameters for each water quality
. defining what waste treatment to carry out

134

- financial: . capital cost, operating costs and maintenance costs
  . corresponding financing plans
- administrative and
  political: . deciding whether the desired objectives (uses) are too ambitious
  . consulting the public through Comités de Patronage for the schemes
  . presentation to the regional political assemblies.

In the Severn-Trent, the desired objectives are also reflected in the way in which water management policy is planned. The policy includes protecting and developing the use of zones of good quality water while improving the zones of poorer quality water. To this end action is taken to control industrial abstractions so as to substitute whenever possible water which is all of inferior quality for that of good quality, i.e. potable water (300,000 m3/day should be substituted in this way). There are even plans to charge industries at differential rates for the two types of supply (untreated water and potable water), as is done in France. The aim is to reuse degraded water along the same watercourse (thorough treatment of urban and industrial discharges, R & D work on the most advanced treatment methods, construction of storm-sewage, lagooning and aeration tanks, and recharging aquifers). As part of this scheme an artificial lake is planned to provide final treatment downstream from Birmingham on the River Tame, whereby 40 per cent of the residual BOD and 70 per cent of the suspended solids would be eliminated after standing for five days. There would be similar treatment for the peak levels of pollution in the first waves of storm-sewage which might stand for half a day and contain considerable non-point polluting discharges. One further type of objective for which special measures are taken is to improve the conditions for treating potable water. Apart from the arrangements for recharging aquifers, it seems to be accepted that the water to be treated should be left to settle in storage tanks before elimination of ammoniacal nitrogen, coagulation and softening, sedimentation and filtration, correction of the pH, absorption onto activated carbon and then disinfection with chlorine.

In the Yodo Basin, the objectives of water management policy are to improve water quality and protect the environment. For this purpose an integrated management of water resources is practised which includes:

- monitoring household and industrial discharges
- construction of waste water disposal and treatment facilities
- trying to make rational use of the land.

In pursuance of these points special efforts are made in four directions, while allowing for a degree of regional development:
- to supply enough water to satisfy a growing demand, mainly by constructing storage dams and recycling waste water;
- to control pollution by damage compensation payments and developing waste water disposal and treatment facilities;
- to achieve an acceptable level for the risks of non-point pollution and the risks of an increase in flooding by regulating land uses;
- to seek a balance between upstream and downstream water uses in a river basin.

Plans for achieving the various objectives of water management policy have already been discussed to some extent in the preceding paragraphs.

Most of the case studies however stress the importance of knowing whether the objectives are attainable with the financial resources available. Here there is genuine competition between carrying out a water management policy and pursuing the goal of economic expansion.

In the Delaware River Basin the improvement observed in profile of dissolved oxygen concentration suffered a setback in 1976. This relapse is perhaps without significance as the environment has in any case been improved by all the efforts made, but it reflects the fact that two important centres, Philadelphia and Camden, New Jersey, are not yet in compliance with their discharge standards. The estimated costs of carrying out an overall waste water treatment programme for the basin was $270 million in 1964, but today it far exceeds $1 billion, because the concept of pollution has become wider and the targets have been set higher.

This increase in costs is general. In the Trent River Basin it is pointed out, a considerable effort will be needed for renewing and increasing pollution control installations.

In the Seine-Normandy area it is estimated that the current rate of expenditure would have to be multiplied by 1.5 or 2 for a comparably increased effort.

In Japan there is still much to be done, especially in the Kyoto area and in the fast-growing satellite towns of Hirakata (whose population increased by 37 per cent in 5 years) and Takatsuki (43 per cent growth in the same period). The following table shows how low the sewer-service rate still is.

Economic reasons and the growing constraint imposed by development are driving countries such as Australia to use less expensive methods than treating effluent in plants followed by discharge into rivers. For example, the policy for developing the Parramatta Basin is based entirely on the construction of sewer systems connected to outlets in the sea which cost about one-fifth as much as treatment in plants discharging purified waste water nearby, i.e. into a river. The additional step might even be taken, again for economic reasons, of encouraging new industries to choose sites on the seacoast.

Table VIII.1

Present state of sewer-service in Yodo River Basin
(as of March 1977)

	Total population (A)	Population serviced by sewer systems (B)	Sewer-service rate (B/A)%
Kyoto City	1,455,813	700,260	48.1
Otsu City	191,474	38,690	20.1
Kirakata City	312,903	91,400	29.2
Takatsuki City	336,212	42,560	12.7

Note: 1. The data are taken from each city.
2. The population serviced by sewer systems in Otsu City is estimated from the area serviced by such systems.

In this case, the main obstacle to carrying out plans effectively for improving water resources is the economic constraint involved in trying to satisfy all the requirements of regional development at once.

But there are also technically complex difficulties which stand in the way of integrated water management.

The first is the increasing difficulty of river training in basins which are becoming more and more industrialised and in which the demand for water is growing, low-water levels are more critical, the risks of flooding are greater whereas the number of possible sites for storage dams is dwindling. The latter is the main difficulty in the basins of rivers such as the Yodo (Japan), the Trent (United Kingdom, where pumped storage in flat land is envisaged), or the Oise (France).

A second difficulty is the inadequate knowledge of water pollution and purification processes (micro-pollutants).

There is also the widely experienced difficulty of extending pollution control measures to cover accidental (momentary) and non-point (continuous) pollution. In addition to agricultural discharges, which are little known, there are others, especially urban run-off and overflows from combined or separate storm sewer systems (as in the Delaware Basin and in the Seine Basin including Paris).

Further difficulties are raised by the treatment of sludge. There are objections to incinerating or dumping it and its disposal is a problem in the Delaware, Seine-Normandy and Trent Basins. For

137

example, what will be done with the sludge which accumulates in the lagooning tanks after the final treatment stage?

These various scientific and technical difficulties show the need for a wider variety of measures for supporting pollution control or the quantitative improvement of water resources. The following diagrams apply to the Seine-Normandy Basin and give an idea of the variety and complexity of operations to be performed simultaneously (Figure 8.1):

Figure 8.1

PERCENTAGE DISTRIBUTION OF POLLUTION CONTROL COMMITMENTS 1977-1981 BY TYPE OF OPERATION (EXCLUDING TREATMENT BONUSES)
POURCENTAGE DE REPARTITION DES ENGAGEMENTS POLLUTION 1977-1981 PAR TYPE D'ACTIONS (HORS PRIMES D'EPURATION

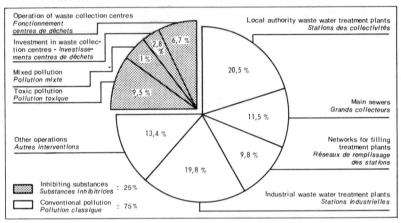

Cost of assisted works - *Montant des travaux aidés :* MF 3 783 (M$ 760)
Aid payments from the Agence de Bassin - *Aides de l'Agence de Bassin* : MF 1 457 (M$ 293)

Figure 8.2

DISTRIBUTION OF RESOURCES COMMITTED 1977-1981 BY TYPE OF OPERATION
REPARTITION DES ENGAGEMENTS «RESSOURCES» 1977-1981 PAR TYPE D'ACTIONS

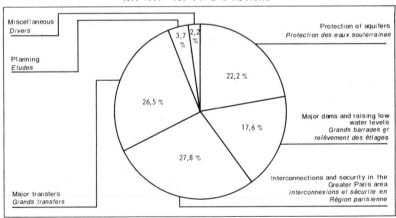

Cost of assisted works - *Montant des travaux aidés :* MF 1 287 (M$ 259)
Aid payments from the Agence de Bassin - *Aides de l'Agence de Bassin* : MF 692 (M$ 139)

4. Adaptation of administrative structures to hydrological realities

In general this adaptation seems to have been made. Although the administrations which have been involved cannot solve all the problems (e.g. because of financial reasons and technological limitations), they have the merit of studying their nature and importance thoroughly.

Thus in the Yodo Basin, the administration tries:

- to fix an exact timetable for achieving quantified objectives
- to draw up a system of standards for limiting polluting discharges
- to supplement these standards at regional level through action by the Prefectures
- to tighten up the limitations on certain polluting parameters for specified industries
- to construct waste water disposal and treatment systems
- to deal with the Liaison Committees on a basis of trust.

In the Severn Trent River Basin in the United Kingdom efforts are being made to adapt technology to the changing situation as regards water quality. It is planned to modify the discharge standards so as to take account of their effects on the natural environment and on the desired quality objectives.

Another attempt at adaptation was more administrative in nature and consisted in the creation in the Trent River Authority of a Quality Monitoring Section for examining discharges from the treatment facilities run by the Authority itself. This Section is a semi-independent body and reports its findings to the Advisory Board on Water Quality which is in contact with the public. Thanks to this arrangement the Authority avoids being judge in its own cause.

One of the methods most often used for measuring how well the administrative structures and the plans they carry out have been adapted to present and future hydrological realities is to work out models for simulating various possible patterns of development.

The conclusions reached with these models are admittedly not sufficiently definite and reliable for decision making, but they provide food for thought and are a factor in changing administrative behaviour.

In the United States a mathematical model was constructed for analysing water quality in the Delaware estuary which was of help in launching the policy of the Delaware River Basin Commission. Although its mathematics are complicated, it was found to oversimplify representation of the biochemical processes. Nevertheless it provided an operational basis for the administration's discussions with the polluters, which were an indispensable stage in bringing the two sides together.

The model formed the base of the pyramid shown in Figure 8.2.

Figure 8.3

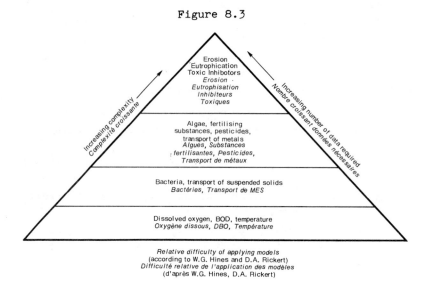

Relative difficulty of applying models
(according to W.G. Hines and D.A. Rickert)
Difficulté relative de l'application des modèles
(d'après W.G. Hines, D.A. Rickert)

The same applies to a model for waste assimilative capacity developed in France in connection with the policy for quality objectives in the Oise River Basin.

The latter model is based on the Streeter and Phelps equations, also used in the Delaware River Basin.

Waste load (BOD): L_t: Lo 10^{-k1t} (L: waste load)

Oxygen deficit: $D_t = Lo \dfrac{k1(10^{-k2t} - 10^{-k1t})}{K_1 - K_2} + Do\ 10^{-K2t}$

(k_1 and k_2: technical co-efficients) (D: oxygen deficit)
With this model it is possible to measure the effects of the discharges and find the oxygen profiles.

The model has been used for calculating the maximum permissible polluting discharges and the effects of the dams on water quality (see figure 8.3).

This programme has been adapted for the estuary of the Seine in conditions comparable to those governing the model for the Delaware.

A more complete technico-economic model was made in the Trent River Basin in the United Kingdom which could simulate four kinds of water demand and different variants of development up to the year 2000. The actual demand for water has proved to be below the model's forecasts, but it has nevertheless provided the River Authority with valuable data.

Two comparable experiments were made in the Seine-Normandy River Basin, one with the POPOLE model for water quality (policy for water pollution) and the other with the POTAME model giving a more

Figure 8.4

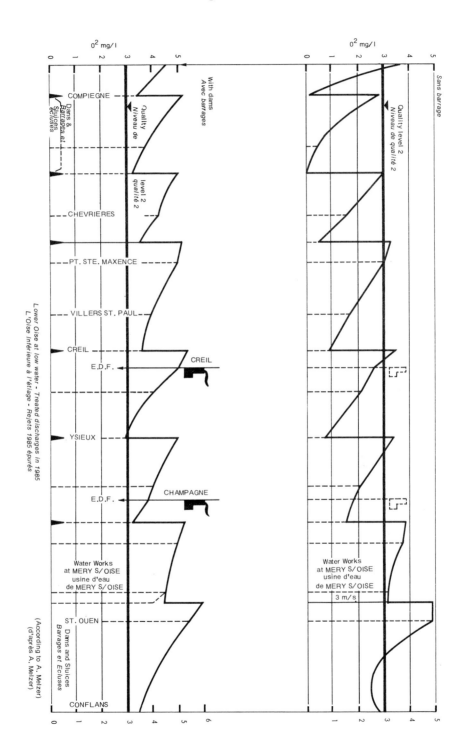

developed and quantified picture (technological policy for water management). The POPOLE model with its 92 variables enabled the political, administrative, financial and technical options to be selected which were of most importance in carrying out the plans of the Agence Financière de Bassin (river basin financing agency). It did not provide a solution for specific problems, but it gave clear indications regarding the adaptability of the Agence as an administrative entity. The model was based on the technique of structural analysis.

The POTAME model is still being tested. It has 149 technical and economic variables and its purpose is to simulate several types of integrated water management, both quantitative and qualitative, and to assess the ability of different policies to stand up to disturbances under the various types of regional development which can be envisaged.

TECHNICAL ANNEX ON POLLUTION CHARGES

Only two countries, France and the Netherlands, make any sys-
tematic use of water pollution charges on a large scale. The com-
parative study appearing in Part B of Chapter III is therefore somewhat limited, since it is only based on the monographs for the Seine-
Normandy and Dommel/Aa basins.

For easier reading of the material in Chapter III and to avoid
any disproportionate treatment compared with the overall study of industrialised basin management, it was believed best to incorporate in
an annex a number of practical details regarding the actual daily
application of charges. Some of the information does not appear in
the case studies used as a basis for drafting the present report.
In view of the newness of the material and its sometimes relatively
complex nature, for purposes of clarity it was decided that it should
follow Chapter III, which it expands in greater depth.

A.   Additional information concerning the pollution charge concept

As stated in section III.B.1, the essential aim of pollution
charges is to provide financial resources for acting to control pollution. They should not be confused with sewerage taxes, which usually are municipal (and not levied by a basin or river authority).
Sewerage taxes are generally rather heavy, and provide for the upkeep
and extension of sewer systems in towns and industrial zones.(1)
They are widely used (unlike pollution charges) and are found in
nearly all the countries covered by this report. As an example, in
the Dommel and Aa basins the sewerage tax amounts to some D.Fl.100
per year and per dwelling. This may be set against the 3.5 x Fl.22 =
Fl.77, the cost of the pollution charge for a household of 3.5 persons.

In France the sewerage tax often reaches Frs.200 per year for a
household (whereas the average pollution charge only amounts to
Frs.40.

Nor should the pollution charge be confused with the abstraction
and consumption charge or water-control charge, corresponding to the
cost for quantitatively managing the water resource. This second

1) A sewer system does not treat but merely conveys pollution. The
    sewerage tax therefore does not directly affect pollution control.

type of charge is described in Chapter IV. For purposes of comparison with the previous indications, the water-control charge in the
Dommel and Aa basins varies between D.Fl.15 and 25 per household per
year, while in the Seine-Normandy basin the abstraction charges
amounts to some Frs.10 to 15 per household per year.

Overall, a comparison of water charges (added to the price of
water, which is not dealt with here) shows the following:

Table A.1

ORDER OF MAGNITUDE OF WATER CHARGES PER HOUSEHOLD
PER YEAR IN THE SEINE-NORMANDY AND DOMMEL-AA BASINS

(US $)	Seine-Normandy	Dommel/Aa
Pollution charge	8	31.3
Sewerage tax	40.3	40.6
Abstraction charge Water control charge	2.5	8.1
Total	50.8	80.0

These figures may be compared with the $150 paid on average for
the price of water per household per year.(1) The charges therefore
amount to one-third of the price of water in the Seine-Normandy basin
and to half in the Dommel-Aa basin

B.   Additional information concerning the assessment basis

The population-equivalent is a convenient unit used in the Seine-
Normandy and Dommel-Aa basins for reckoning pollution. It is however
differently defined.

Table A.2
POPULATION EQUIVALENT (GRAMS PER DAY)

	Seine-Normandy	Dommel-Aa
Suspended solids	90(1)	(120 p.m)
Oxidisable substances COD	-	135
OM (oxidisable matter)(2)	57	-
Nitrogenous substances N	p.m.	10(3)
Total adopted	147 or 102	180

1) May be assigned a weighting coefficient of $\frac{1}{2}$.
2) OM $= \frac{COD}{3} + \frac{2BOD_5}{3}$
3) Assigned a weighting coefficient of 4.57

1) Hypotheses: 300 litres of water per inhabitant and per household
    (including municipal services and small establishments); 3.5 per-
    sons per household; 40 US cents per m³ of water sold to inhabitants

144

In the Dommel/Aa basin the assessment basis adopted for pollution is a _flow_ of oxidisable substances:

$$W_o = Q \frac{COD + 4.57 N}{180}$$

Where Q is the amount discharged per 24 hours (in m^3)

COD and N are concentrations (in mg/l)

W is without unity, in population equivalents for toxic substances

W_t = A in kgs of suspended solids discharged per year

$W_S = \frac{D-60\,Wo}{120}$, where D is the number of grams per day of sludge

(dry weight) discharged.

W_o is the flow of oxidisable matter. If the effluent comes from treatment plant, W_o should be replaced by:

$$W_e = \frac{2.5 \ BOD_5 + 4.57N}{180}$$

BOD_5 being expressed in mg/l.

In the Seine-Normandy Basin very similar formulas are used. Flows are likewise involved. It is however preferred to keep the assessments in the form of kgs per day rather than convert to population equivalents. In calculating the assessment basis the following factors are included:

- suspended solids (SS) in g or kg per day
- oxidisable matter (OM) expressed by a weighted average of chemical oxygen demand and biochemical oxygen demand over five days in g or kg per day:

$$OM = \frac{COD + 2BOD_5}{3}$$

- soluble salts, expressed by conductivity multiplied by the volume of water discharged (mho/cm) x m^3
- inhibiting and toxic substances, evaluated by means of a biological test (based on the reactions of a small shellfish, the daphnia). The measuring unit is the equitox-gram/day or equitox-kilogram day.

The measurement of inhibiting and toxic substances consists in assessing the effects these produce on a population of daphnias. The proportion of deaths is a nearly linear function of the concentration of the toxic solution. By gradually diluting the latter a concentration in which 50 per cent of the daphnias die is obtained, one regarded as normal. The number of times the initial sample has had to be diluted indicates the _equitox_ number for the solution.

Figure A.1

CALCULATION OF EQUITOX NUMBER IN THE
SEINE-NORMANDY BASIN

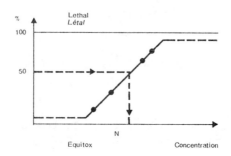

Different rates are applied to the four preceding terms, with
the result that the charges are given by a linear combination of the
type:

$$R = t_{SS} \times SS + t_{OM} \times OM$$
$$\text{(francs)} \quad \text{(Fr/kg/day)} \quad \text{(kg/day)} \quad \text{(Fr/kg/day)} \quad \text{(kg/day)}$$

$$+ t_{Salt} \times Salt + t_{IS}$$
$$\text{(Fr/mho/cm x m}^3) \quad \text{(mho/cm x m}^3) \quad \text{(Fr/equitox/gr/day)}$$

$$\times IS$$
$$\text{(equitox/gr/day)}$$

Unlike the Dommel-Aa formula it does not take nitrogenous substances into account, but the question of including them is very much
alive.

By taking only the first two terms (SS and OM), which are valid
for household wastes and non-toxic and non-saline industrial wastes,
like for the Dommel-Aa basin the assessment basis for the charges can
also be expressed in population equivalents.

Up to 1976 the financial rates for suspended solids and oxidisable matter were the same. A town dweller was assumed to discharge
90 grams per day of SS and 57 grams per day of OM, so that:

$$A = \frac{SS + OM}{147}$$
$$\text{(p.e.)} \quad \text{(gr/day)}$$

After that it was decided to allow for the higher cost of destroying oxidisable matter discharged by industrialists by applying
twice the rate for oxidisable matter in the Seine-Normandy Basin
(tripling the rate is even now being discussed):

146

$$t_{OM} = 2\ t_{SS}$$
$$(\mathrm{Fr/gr/day})$$

In terms of population equivalents the assessment basis A thus becomes in this case:

$$A = \frac{OM + \dfrac{SS}{2}}{102}$$
$$\text{(p.e.)} \qquad \text{(gr/day)}$$

OM and SS being expressed in grams per day (giving $57 + \dfrac{90}{2} = 102$ for a town dweller).

Although for purposes of comparison a sewerage rather than a pollution charge is strictly involved, the following formula used by the Trent River Authority should be of interest:

$$C = R + V + \frac{O_t}{O_s}\, B + \frac{S_t}{S_s}\, S$$

where C = charge in pence per m^3 of industrial effluent

R = 1/3 of the average cost of collecting and conveying the effluents to the treatment plant, in pence/m^3

V = average annual cost of primary and volumetric treatment of effluents, in pence/m^3

O_t = COD (in mg/l) of effluent

O_s = average annual value of COD in mg/l

B = average annual cost of biological treatment per m^3

S_t = SS (in mg/l) of effluent

S_s = annual mean value of suspended solids in mg/l

S = average annual cost of treatment of suspended solids (per m^3)

The previous linear combinations, by applying rates expressed in monetary terms to pollutant flows (or concentrations), show what amounts should be paid.

In order to avoid measuring the various flows (or concentrations) in the case of small polluting sources, recourse is had to flat-rate estimates for each activity.

Such estimates can either relate a pollution discharge value expressed in terms of its various components (SS, OM, toxic substances, salts) to a convenient unit (number of workers in a plant, amount of goods produced), or else be directly (as in the Dommel-Aa case) expressed in population equivalents.

If a_i is the estimated amount of pollution by each activity and
    k_i is the size of the activity
    the estimated pollution by an enterprise with n activities will be:

$$W = \sum_{i = 1}^{n} k_i\, a_i$$

Examples of this type of calculation will be found in later pages.

In calculating the charges, the method of discharging the effluent may be taken into account. In the Dommel-Aa basin a volume correction factor is then applied. The discharge rate Q previously used is then corrected by the coefficient:

$$V_c = \frac{Q - Q_s}{50}$$

where Q is a standard volume of water annually discharged.

Q_s is regarded as equal to 25 m^3, i.e. 250 working days multiplied by 100 litres per day.

According to the value of Q, the correction provided by V_c may be positive or negative.

If 45 per cent or more of the discharge occurs at night, then the correction becomes:

$$V_c = \frac{0.8 \ Q - Q_s}{50}$$

C.   Calculating the rate of charge

It has been explained how the total amount of charges balances out with that of expenditure programmes (see section III.B.3).

Use in the Dommel-Aa basin of a single unit for assessing the basis (the population equivalent) results in a single determination of the rate. If M is the amount to be covered in the investment programme (see Table III.3), W is the amount of pollution discharged in population equivalents and t the rate of the assessment basis unit, then:

$$t = \frac{M}{W}$$

In the Seine-Normandy basin, determination of the rates is more complex owing to the greater number of parameters adopted.

As the value of M in the programme and its duration (in years) are known, we have:

$$M = t_{ss} \sum_1^n (SS)_i + t_{OM} \sum_1^n (OM)_i + t_{salt} \ x \sum_1^n (salt)_i + t_{is} \sum_1^n (IS)_i$$

(in francs)

$$\text{with } t_{SS} = \frac{t_{OM}}{2}$$

There may be financially balanced subprogrammes (as for "salinity" and "toxicity") which make it possible to select t_{salt} and t_{IS}.

While this calculation is based on a sound principle, it is in fact slightly more complex for two reasons:

- the summation $\sum_1^n$ for the n years of an action programme can be continued over a greater number of years (e.g. $\sum_1^{n+2}$), which makes it possible to reduce the values of the rates slightly. Charges not levied by the end of programme M will of course have to be carried forward and debited to the following programme so as to keep it in overall balance.
- the river basin financing agencies make no clearcut distinction between the pollution charges discussed here and charges for abstraction and consumption (see Chapter IV).

Hence the above-mentioned redistribution balance should be widened:

M_{global} (pollution plus resource improvement) = $t_{average}$ pollution x pollution base + $t_{average}$ abstractions x abstraction base

(Francs) = (Fr/suitable unit) x (suitable units) + (Fr/m^3) x (m^3)

Although a sewerage tax rather than a pollution charge is involved, the rates indicated for certain sewerage and treatment functions would seem worth applying to the formula used in the Trent River basin:

R
(collection and conveyance) = 1.19 p/m^3 ($0.2)

(at £.587 = US$1)

V
(primary treatment) = 3.28 p/m^3 ($0.55)

B
(biological treatment) = 2.64 p/m^3 ($0.45)

S
(sludge) = 1.21 p/m^3 ($0.2)

Taking population equivalent as close to 300 litres/day (from the point of view of drainage and waste treatment capacity), i.e., about 100 m^3/year, the above figures become:

for 1 p.e.
{
1/3 collection and conveyance: $2
primary treatment : $5.5
biological treatment : $4.5
sludge treatment : $2
} $14/year

A charge of $49 per year per household is therefore obtained, which is compatible with the values for sewerage taxes and pollution charges shown in Table III.13 of section A.

D.   Redistribution from charges in the Seine-Normandy Basin

The following are the sums estimated to be collected and to be redistributed for the Seine-Normandy River Basin Agency during the 1977-81 action programme, everything balancing out:

Figure A.2

REDISTRIBUTION OF REVENUE FROM POLLUTION CHARGES (SEINE-NORMANDY)
REDISTRIBUTION DES PRODUITS DES REDEVANCES DE POLLUTION (SEINE-NORMANDIE)

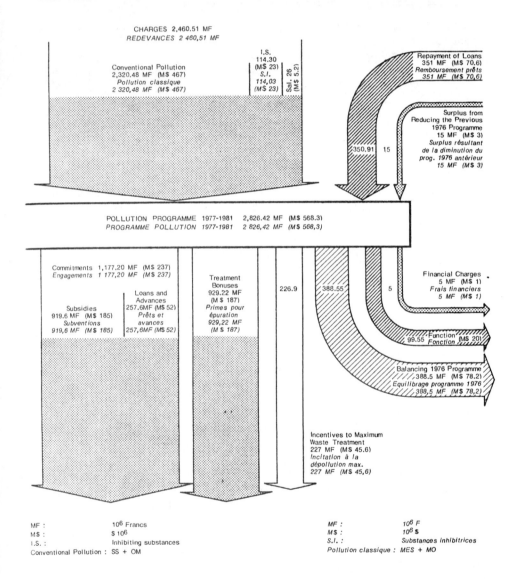

The straight unhatched arrows represent the main financial resources and uses. They correspond either to a technical assessment
basis (quantity of pollution discharged into the river) or capital
and operating expenditure of pollution control plants. The curved
hatched arrows represent financial balancing transactions without
technical counterpart (accounting for surpluses and overspending on
previous programmes).

As may be seen, most of the revenue from the charges is used
for meeting commitments and paying bonuses for waste treatment and
maximum pollution reduction.

D.1 The commitments (see Figure A.2) are to finance new investment /waste treatment plant, drainage works, changeover to less polluting industrial processes(1) etc.7. They are discharged by paying
subsidies (usually 30 per cent of the cost of the works involved)
and by granting loans and advances repayable in ten years at reasonable rates of interest (about 9 per cent). The loans range from
10 per cent of the total cost of the works (when a municipality is
assisted by a river basin financing agency) to 20 per cent of the
cost of the works (in the case of assisted industries) (see
Table III.6, section III.B.4).

Thus in the case of industries the aids granted amount to
30+20 = 50 per cent of the cost of the works. This is not direct
aid from the public authorities to industrial establishments, but
is a redistribution of the contributions from polluting water users
in a river basin through the river basin financing agency operating
as a compensation and equalisation fund. Moreover, particular attention is given in order to limit economic transfers between categories of users (in particular industries and municipalities). Thus
financial aids approximately and globally balance charges for each
category of user.

This mutual aid or co-operative system also operates for municipalities, but to a lesser extent, because only 30+10 = 40 per cent
of the cost of works is assisted. In this case the public authorities, acting through the Ministry of Agriculture or the Ministry of
the Interior, provide a subsidy of 30 per cent for controlling pollution. Region and Département (equivalent to a County) subsidies increase the aid by 10 per cent, (see Table III.7).

Thus the sums redistributed by the river basin agency average
about 45 per cent of the cost of works carried out for controlling

---

1) These industrial processes are assisted to the extent of the
   financial outlay which would otherwise be needed to build a
   treatment plant.

conventional pollution. These works therefore are estimated to cost about Frs.1,962 million for the period 1977-1981 ($395 million over five years) on the understanding that conventional pollutions accounts for Frs.883 million of the total commitments of Frs.1,177 million (Frs.1,962 million x 45 per cent = Frs.883 million paid by the agency).

Most of the aid payments for controlling inhibiting and toxic substances (Frs.1,177-883 million = Frs.294 million) are moreover distributed to industrialists on varying terms and conditions.

A conditional subsidy of 50 per cent is granted together with a loan of 20 per cent repayable over 10 years with interest at 9 per cent per annum. The subsidy is granted subject to monitoring of the the results obtained. Monitoring takes place after the detoxication installations have been completed. If the result is poor, the subsidy must be refunded to the river basin agency.

Assistance is also given for controlling sludge and wastes in the form of a loan covering 50 per cent of the expenditure incurred in constructing centres for destroying and recovering wastes.

The aid granted for these operations averages about 60 per cent of their cost, so that the cost of works for controlling toxic pollution and wastes are estimated to amount to Frs.490 million ($98.6 million) for the period in question (1977/81) (Frs.490 million x 60 per cent = Frs.294 million).

As a result the Frs.1,117 million worth of commitments are generating Frs.2,452 million ($493 million) worth of works (Frs.1,962 million + 490 million = Frs.2,452 million).

The distribution of these financial aids is programmed.

As regards the procedure for allocating aid payments, the applications with their technical specifications are forwarded to the river basin financing agency for consideration, and after being processed are submitted to committees of the agency's board of management which make the decision.

Consideration of applications includes assessing not only their technical soundness, but also the cost of the schemes they propose, and the latter are only approved if they come within the financial ceiling. In 1976 the capital cost of plant for treating conventional pollution was not to exceed the values shown in Table A.3.

Table A.3

MAXIMUM CEILINGS FOR INTERVENTION OF THE SEINE-NORMANDY AGENCY (1976)

Conventional Pollution	Small treatment stations (from 0 to 1,000 inhabs.)	Medium-sized treatment stations (from 1,000 to 5,000 inhabitants)	Large treatment stations (9,000 inhabitants and over)
Ceiling for allowing aid payments	300 Frs./pe ($60.3/pe)	250 Frs./pe ($50.3/pe)	180 Frs./pe ($36.2/pe)
Industrial treatment stations	2040 Frs./kg/d ($410.5/kg/d)	1700 Frs./kg/d ($342/kg/d)	1225 Frs./kg/d ($246.5/kg/d)

1 kg/day = 6.8 pe
1 pe = 0.147 kg of pollutants (SS + OM)

These ceilings may be increased by from 30 to 40 per cent in the case of more thorough treatment (nitrification - denitrification and disinfection of effluents).

For toxic and inhibiting pollutants there is a ceiling on aid of Frs.45 per equitox gram/day (or Frs.45,000, i.e. $9,054, per equitox kg/day).

It will be seen from these various particulars that a special effort is made to control toxic pollution; charges on toxic pollutants are less than 5 per cent of the total revenue from charges, whereas the financial aids granted are not quite 2.5 per cent of total aid payments.

The ceiling applied to aids for constructing conventional waste treatment stations is from 18 to 30 times higher than the corresponding charge (Frs.10/p.e.), whereas the ceiling for plant controlling toxic pollution is 45 times higher than the charge on toxic pollutants (Frs.1/equitox/g).

D.2 Bonuses for waste treatment and incentives to maximum pollution control concern the operation, i.e. the maintenance and running of pollution control works.

Bonuses for waste treatment are refunds to municipalities of their expenditure on the waste treatment plants they operate. The refunds depend on the technical efficiency of these stations. Teams of technical assistants who are paid half by the river basin agency and half by the Département authorities are responsible for measuring their technical efficiency.

Let us take a municipality of n inhabitants whose pollution P is discharged directly into a river. If the rate of charge is t, the sum R paid to the river basin agency will be R = P.t.

Per inhabitant the amount due will be: $r = \frac{P}{N} t$.

This sum will be included in the water bill paid by each water user to the (municipal or private) water supply company, which will transfer it (the counterpart of pollution by domestic and similar water users) to the river basin agency.

Let us now assume that the municipality has a waste treatment station which operates with an efficiency k. The total pollution discharged into the river will then be (1-k) P and the charge which should be paid will be R = (1-k) P.t. The river basin agency will be paid the equivalent of P.t and should therefore refund to the municipality the sum of S = kPt, which is the <u>waste treatment bonus.</u> This bonus will be returned to the water users, for example by reducing the rates (a reduction of $\frac{kPt}{n}$ for each rate payer) or by using the bonus to meet municipal expenditure which will then not be charged to local tax revenue.

Accordingly, in Figure A.2 showing how the revenue from pollution charges is redistributed, the waste treatment bonuses totalling Frs.929.2 million ($187 million) represent the excess pollution charges levied in the total of Frs.2,460.5 million ($495 million).

Therefore the <u>net</u> charges actually paid by the polluters amount to Frs.1,531.3 million ($308 million) (Frs.2,460.5 million - 929.2 million = Frs.1,531.3 million).

The case of industrialists is different. No waste treatment bonus is paid, because the emission charges are calculated on the quality of pollutants discharged into the river after treatment, so that the river basin agency collects the net value of the charges directly.

Another type of financial redistribution scheme connected with operating conditions consists in giving incentive aid to <u>maximise pollution control.</u> It applies both to municipalities and to industries who make a special effort to optimise the operation of their waste treatment plant with the help and advice of Département technical assistance teams.

The principle behind this aid is to relieve polluters of some of the operating expenses they have to bear (usually amounting to about 10 per cent per year of the capital cost of their waste treatment stations).

The incentive bonus paid depends:

(a) on the estimated running cost given by a scale varying with the capacity of the station. Separate figures are given for removing suspended solids (SS) and removing oxidisable matter (OM).

(b) the station's load factor, i.e. the ratio between the pollution actually entering it and its nominal capacity. A load of under 50 per cent disqualifies for financial aid, while full loading increases it by a factor of 1.5.

154

(c) the station's efficiency in removing SS and OM. Financial support (maximum 45 per cent and minimum 25 per cent) is calculated from these efficiency factors on condition that they are higher than 60 per cent for SS and 50 per cent for OM.

As an example, the maximum aid granted to a fully loaded (load factor = 100 per cent) station of 1,000,000 pe and with a SS efficiency of 90 per cent and an OM efficiency of 80 per cent amounts to

$$
\begin{array}{l}
= 1.5 \left[\underset{\substack{SS \\ co- \\ effi- \\ cient}}{0.40} \times \underset{Frs./kg/day}{26.8} \times \underset{kg/day}{90,000} + \underset{\substack{OM \\ Co- \\ effi- \\ cient}}{0.37} \times \underset{\substack{Frs./ \\ kg/ \\ day}}{80.3} \times \underset{kg/day}{57,000} \right] \neq Frs.4 \text{ million} \\
\text{Aid}
\end{array}
$$

Thus in this case the support given by the agency accounts for about Frs.4 million out of the Frs.7 million which the waste treatment station costs to run. This rate of participation (57 per cent) may be regarded as an upper limit.

For industrial waste treatment stations the conditions are more strict. There is no financial aid, and no support payment unless the load factor is 100 per cent. The coefficients in regard to SS and OM are smaller.

For a station of the same size, an equivalent calculation to the preceding one would give a support payment of slightly less than Frs.0.5 million, i.e. a participation of about 7 per cent in operating costs.

During the period to which the financial incentive programme applies, incentive payments for maximum pollution control are made up to the total estimated sum (Frs.227 million or \$45.6 million in Figure A.2).

The economic justification for these special subsidies is that they provide an incentive supplementing emission charges, when for reasons of public policy the rates for the latter are not fixed high enough.

Let us take a polluter who directly discharges an amount of untreated pollutants P. He should pay a charge of $R = P.t$, where t is the rate of charge. Let us now suppose that he has a waste treatment station of efficiency k. He will then pay a charge of $R' = (1-k)Pt$, but will have to meet operating costs of $F = P.t_F$, where t_F is the cost of operating the station.

If the charge is to be incentive (disregarding any regulations which oblige the polluter to treat his wastes), it is necessary for:

$$(1-k)Pt + P.t_F < Pt$$

i.e. it must be cheaper to treat the wastes than to pollute.
In this case it is necessary for $t > \dfrac{t_F}{k}$

If k = 80 per cent and t_F = 80 F/kg/d (average running cost of a plant of 10,000 pe), then

$$t > Frs.100/kg/day$$

At present the basic rate of charge in Seine-Normandy is only some Frs.100.

The incentive effect is increased by introducing an incentive aid payment to maximise pollution control. The previous inequality then becomes:

$$(1-k)Pt + Pt_F - A < Pt$$

If A is written in the form A = Pa (where A = aid and a = the rate of aid) the incentive conditions are lightened:

$$t > \frac{t_F - a}{k}$$

Thus more satisfactory economic incentives are obtained without having to raise the charges. Of course this system of financial redistribution which lowers running costs rather than helping new investment results in slowing down the programme for providing plant. From Figure 3.4 the delay may be estimated at:

$$\frac{Frs.227\ m}{Frs.1,117\ m + Frs.227\ m} = 16\ \text{per cent, or one year out of six}$$

E.   Examples in computing the charges

Industrial effluents must be distinguished from household effluents.

Industrial effluents

Generally speaking it would be too expensive to take direct measurements for calculating the assessment basis of charges, because too many would be required. Use might of course be made of a decentralised system of controlled individual measurements (such systems are found in the United States and Sweden). In the Seine-Normandy and Dommel-Aa basins, however, flat-rate assessment, enabling simpler indicators for calculating the basis to be used, is preferred.

In the Seine-Normandy Basin an estimate is made from a scale which depends on the industry, the process and the type of product. For each unit of output (e.g. one tonne of steel, one tonne of tanned hides or one livestock unit) the scale gives the quantity of pollutants produced theoretically, expressed in SS, OM, inhibiting substances and salinity.

Taking the case of a tannery (making leather from cattle hides) with an output of 9,400 tonnes of hides in 1976 and 41 tonnes/day in the month of peak activity (the appropriate period for calculating the charges), the calculation gives the following figures:

Table A.4

EXTRACT FROM DISCHARGE ESTIMATES:
TANNERIES IN THE SEINE-NORMANDY BASIN

Indicator	SS (kg/d)	MO (kg/d)	I.S. Equitox-gram	Salinity Mho
1 tonne of hides	70	50	2500	0

For the selected example (41 tonnes/day of pollution discharged):

SS	2,870 kg/day	x Frs.38	=	Frs.109,060
OM	2,050 kg/day	x Frs.78	=	Frs.155,800
IS	102,500 Eq_x	x Frs. 0.8	=	Frs. 82,000
Salts	0	x Frs.1,350	=	0

Frs.346,860

For purposes of illustration (and comparison) the pollution produced by this tannery was in fact measured in 1976 with the following result:

SS	7,739 kg	x	Frs.38	=	Frs.294,082
OM	3,767 kg	x	Frs.76	=	Frs.286,292
IS	22,933 Eq_x	x	Frs. 0.8	=	Frs. 18,346
Salinity	42,590 Mho		the salinity was not counted(1)		

Frs.598,720

1) The reason salinity was not counted is because the discharge occurs in an area where no charge is levied on salinity.

This is an example of the often considerable difference which there may be between applying a "rule-of-thumb" scale which is lenient towards polluters and a much more rigorous and therefore stricter measurement of actual discharges.

Such a scale is used mainly for calculating the charges payable by small point sources of pollution, while the measurement procedure is kept for the few sources of major pollution where the cost of measurement is covered by the difference found between the two estimates of pollution (in the preceding example over Frs.250,000, i.e. almost ten times the cost of measurement).

The scales for industrial pollution are drawn up at national level in agreement with the trade associations. Both the polluters and the public authorities have the right to request the non-application of these scales if they agree to pay for direct measurement, in which case the charges will of course be calculated on the results of the latter (even if they give lower figures than the scale, which rarely happens).

In the Dommel-Aa basin it is also worthwhile to note the result of pollution estimates for a tannery handling 6,000 hides per day.

Suspended solids have been omitted, since they are considered to account for a fairly negligible amount of pollution.

Organic pollution load:

For computing the magnitude of pollution use is made of the formula:

$$W = Q \left(\frac{COD + 4.57\ N}{180}\right)$$

where W   = pollution load (p.e.)
COD = chemical oxygen demand (mg/l)
N   = org. N + (NH$_4$) N-content (mg/l)
Q   = rate of discharge (m^3/day).

The input data make no reference to the N_{kj} content. It is therefore assumed that for a tannery the relationship N/COD = 1/9. Substitution of the relevant data results in:

$$W = 306 \left(\frac{2500 + 4.57 \times 2500/9}{180}\right)$$

$$= \underline{6\ 408\ p.e.}$$

Heavy Metals

For the discharge of heavy metals a pollution load of 1 p.e. needs to be added for every kilogram of metal discharged per year.

The quality of chromium contained in the waste-water - assuming 250 working days each year - amounts to:

250 x 306(m^3/day) x 200(g/m^3) = $\underline{15\ 300\ kg\ Cr/annum.}$

The total pollution load is therefore:

6 408 + 15 300 = $\underline{21\ 708\ p.e.}$

Volume Correction

If the waste-water is conveyed directly to a treatment plant belonging to one of the Waterboards a volume correction - based on 250 working days/year - is applied according to the formula:

$$V_c \qquad \frac{Q - Q_s}{50}$$

where V_c = volume correction (p.e.)
Q = discharge (m^3/annum)
Q_s = standard discharge (m^3/annum)
   = 250(days) x 0.1(m^3/p.e.) x W(p.e.).

However the application of this formula is restricted to effluents with a water content equal to or exceeding 50 l/p.e. per day. For discharges below this threshold, the (negative) volume correction corresponding to this limit will be applicable.

For the tannery considered, the daily water content per p.e. amounts to $306(m^3/day)/21\ 708$ p.e. = <u>14 1/p.e. per day.</u>

Hence, in this case the volume correction will be subject to the restriction referred to above and therefore be based on a (nominal) effluent discharge of:

50(1/p.e. per day) x 21,708(p.e.) = <u>1085.4 m^3/day.</u>

Substitution in the formula gives:

$$V_c = \frac{250 \times 1085.4 - 25 \times 21,708}{50} = \underline{5,427 \text{ p.e.}}$$

Total Pollution Load

The pollution charge will therefore be based on a load of:

pollution load	W =	21,708 p.e.
volume correction	V_c =	(-) 5,427 p.e.
total		16,281 p.e.

For the year 1977 the annual charge for discharging the effluent directly into a treatment plant would have been:

(i) in the region controlled by the River Aa Water Board
16 281 p.e. at 22.32 Dfl./p.e. = <u>Dfl.363,391.92</u>

(ii) in the region controlled by the River Dommel Water Board
16 281 p.e. at 23.04 Dfl./p.e. = <u>Dfl.375,114.24</u>

For discharge of the effluent directly into surface water the corresponding 1977 annual pollution charge would have been:

(i) River Aa Water Board
21 708 p.e. at 22.32 Dfl./p.e. = <u>Dfl.484,522.56</u>

(ii) River Dommel Water Board
21 708 p.e. at 23.04 Dfl./p.e. = <u>Dfl.500,152.32</u>

A comparison of such two evaluations is not easy to make, as the definitions of units vary between systems.

In the Seine-Normandy basin, application of the scale results in a charge of Frs.350,000 for 41 tonnes of hides per day (i.e. Frs.8,500 per tonne of hides). Hence, the rate per population equivalent was (in 1976) Frs.7.72.

In the case of the Dommel-Aa basin, the charge amounts to Dfl.500,000 for 6,000 hides per day, but the charge is six times higher (Dfl.23 per p.e.).

If a hide is assumed to weight 30 kg, the charge per tonne of hide amounts to Dfl.2,800 (Frs.5,600). If account is taken of the variation between the rates of charge (in a ratio of some 1 to 6), the pollution load as estimated according to the French scale would seem much greater (some 9 times) compared with the Netherlands scale. This point should be checked and more thoroughly investigated.

Another example of calculation may be given for an oil refinery (located in the lower valley of the Seine).

Application of the rule of thumb leads to the following operation:

The characteristic magnitude is the labour force: 1,850 staff in 1978
The specific coefficients are respectively SS = 3, OM = 3
The gross assessment basis is therefore: SS = 5,550 kg, OM = 5,550 kg
Hence the gross 1978 charge would be put at Frs.754,743.

Pollution measurements were in fact carried out in 1974. The characteristic magnitude is the tonne of oil refined per day, one easy to measure and monitor. In 1978 the average figure for a month of maximum activity is 53,425 tonnes per day.

The specific coefficients based on a measurement carried out in 1974 were respectively: SS per tonne produced: 63.87 g; OM per tonne: 144.486 g; Equitox per tonne: 5 g.

The gross assessment basis is therefore:

SS = 3412 kg per average day during a month of maximum activity; OM = 7719 kg; Equitox = 267.125.
Hence the rate of the 1978 charge being:
SS/kg = Frs.45.33; OM/kg = Frs.90.66; equitox/kg = Frs.0.954, the net amount of the charge is Frs.1,109,229 for 1978.

A similar calculation has been carried out for a petrochemical facility in the Dommel-Aa basin.

By applying the formula

$$W = Q \quad \frac{COD + 4.57 \ N}{180} \quad \text{for the pollution load,}$$

we obtain:

$$W = 24 \times 975 \ (\frac{2127 + 0}{180}) = 276,510 \text{ p.e.}$$

Hence for levying purposes, the pollution load resulting from the discharge of raw (untreated) waste water amounts to 276,510 p.e.

Volume correction

If this waste-load is conveyed directly (e.g. by means of a trunk-sewer or such like) to a waste-water treatment plant belonging to one of the Waterboards referred to, a volume correction is applied to the pollution load computed above. For a plant discharging 365 days per year the following formula applies:

$$V_c = \frac{Q - Q_s}{(50 \times 365)/250}$$

where V_c = volume correction (p.e.)
Q = discharge (m^3/year)
Q_s = standard discharge (m^3/year).

For this case:

$$Q_s = 365(days) \times 0.1(m^3/sec) \times W(p.e.)$$

As in addition the rate of discharge of effluent is rather uniformly spread over a day (more than 45 per cent of the volume is discharged at night between 7 p.m. and 7 a.m.) the discharge Q may be
multiplied by a conversion factor 0.8.

Substitution of the data supplied results in:

$$V_c = \frac{0.8 \times 8\ 545,340 - 365 \times 0.1 \times 276,510}{73}$$

$$= 44,607 \text{ p.e.}$$

Total Pollution Load

For levying purposes the total pollution load amounts to:

pollution load   W   =   276,510 p.e.
volume correction V_c = (-) 44,607 p.e.
      total   231,903 p.e.

If the effluent of the petrochemical facility is discharged
directly into surface water, no volume correction is applicable and
the pollution charge will be based on a load of 276,510 p.e.

Annual Pollution Charges

For the year 1977 the annual levy for discharging the effluent
directly into a treatment plant would have been:

(i) in the region of the River Aa Water Board
     231,903(p.e.) at 22.32(Dfl./p.e.) = Dfl.5,176,074.96
(ii) in the region of the River Dommel Water Board
     231,903(p.e.) at 23.04(Dfl./p.e.) = Dfl.5,343,045.12

For effluents discharged directly into surface water, the corresponding 1977 annual charges would have been:

(i) River Aa Water Board
     276,510(p.e.) at 22.32(Dfl./p.e.) = Dfl.6,171,703.20
(ii) River Dommel Water Board
     276,510(p.e.) at 23.04(Dfl./p.e.) = Dfl.6,370,790.40

These similar industries might be compared if a few production
features of the latter example were known.

Calculating the charges for municipalities is a simpler process.
In the Seine-Normandy basin the yardstick is the number of town
dwellers.

According to the size of the town, coefficients increasing or· decreasing the rate may be applied to actual numbers of inhabitants (empirical account is taken of the density or spread of inhabitants).

Table A.5

COEFFICIENTS APPLYING TO NUMBERS OF INHABITANTS
SELECTED FOR CALCULATING POLLUTION BY MUNICIPALITIES
IN THE SEINE-NORMANDY

Size of Towns	Coefficients
Towns > 100,000	1.2
15,000 < towns < 100,000	1.2
500 < towns < 15,000	0.5

F.   Long-term programming of rates of charge and amount of pollution
abatement

The principle of such a programme (carried out in the Seine-Normandy basin) is shown in Figure A.3 below. Starting with a forecast of gross pollution (upper line), the pollution discharged (broken line) subject to no further effort of abatement is calculated.

Simulation calculations are made to determine how much pollution would be abated by charging different rates (reckoned in constant francs). An optimal timetable for the work is then deduced.

Figure A.3

EFFICIENCY OF A POLLUTIONCCONTROL PROGRAMME
IN THE SEINE—NORMANDY BASIN

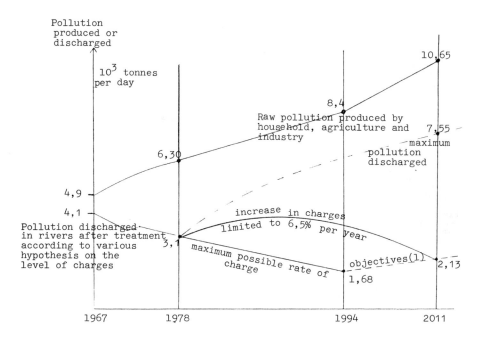

(1) Objectives : 80 % treatment

According to how the charges are revaluated, identical
relative objectives are reached in 1994 or in 2011.

163

OECD SALES AGENTS
DÉPOSITAIRES DES PUBLICATIONS DE L'OCDE

ARGENTINA – ARGENTINE
Carlos Hirsch S.R.L., Florida 165, 4° Piso (Galería Guemes)
1333 BUENOS-AIRES, Tel. 33-1787-2391 Y 30-7122

AUSTRALIA – AUSTRALIE
Australia & New Zealand Book Company Pty Ltd.,
23 Cross Street, (P.O.B. 459)
BROOKVALE NSW 2100   Tel. 938-2244

AUSTRIA – AUTRICHE
Gerold and Co., Graben 31, WIEN 1. Tel. 52.22.35

BELGIUM – BELGIQUE
LCLS
44 rue Otlet, B 1070 BRUXELLES . Tel. 02-521 28 13

BRAZIL – BRÉSIL
Mestre Jou S.A., Rua Guaipà 518,
Caixa Postal 24090, 05089 SAO PAULO 10. Tel. 261-1920
Rua Senador Dantas 19 s/205-6, RIO DE JANEIRO GB.
Tel. 232-07. 32

CANADA
Renouf Publishing Company Limited,
2182 St. Catherine Street West,
MONTREAL, Quebec H3H 1M7 Tel. (514) 937-3519

DENMARK – DANEMARK
Munksgaards Boghandel,
Nørregade 6, 1165 KØBENHAVN K. Tel. (01) 12 85 70

FINLAND – FINLANDE
Akateeminen Kirjakauppa
Keskuskatu 1, 00100 HELSINKI 10. Tel. 65-11-22

FRANCE
Bureau des Publications de l'OCDE,
2 rue André-Pascal, 75775 PARIS CEDEX 16. Tel. (1) 524.81.67
Principal correspondant :
13602 AIX-EN-PROVENCE : Librairie de l'Université.
Tel. 26.18.08

GERMANY – ALLEMAGNE
OECD Publications and Information Centre
4 Simrockstrasse
5300 BONN   Tel. 21 60 46

GREECE – GRÈCE
Librairie Kauffmann, 28 rue du Stade,
ATHÈNES 132. Tel. 322.21.60

HONG-KONG
Government Information Services,
Sales and Publications Office, Beaconsfield House, 1st floor,
Queen's Road, Central.   Tel. 5-233191

ICELAND – ISLANDE
Snaebjörn Jónsson and Co., h.f.,
Hafnarstraeti 4 and 9, P.O.B. 1131, REYKJAVIK.
Tel. 13133/14281/11936

INDIA – INDE
Oxford Book and Stationery Co.:
NEW DELHI, Scindia House. Tel. 45896
CALCUTTA, 17 Park Street. Tel.240832

INDONESIA – INDONÉSIE
PDIN-LIPI, P.O. Box 3065/JKT., JAKARTA, Tel. 583467

ITALY – ITALIE
Libreria Commissionaria Sansoni:
Via Lamarmora 45, 50121 FIRENZE. Tel. 579751
Via Bartolini 29, 20155 MILANO. Tel. 365083
Sub-depositari:
Editrice e Libreria Herder,
Piazza Montecitorio 120, 00 186 ROMA. Tel. 674628
Libreria Hoepli, Via Hoepli 5, 20121 MILANO. Tel. 865446
Libreria Lattes, Via Garibaldi 3, 10122 TORINO. Tel. 519274
La diffusione delle edizioni OCSE è inoltre assicurata dalle migliori
librerie nelle città più importanti.

JAPAN – JAPON
OECD Publications and Information Center
Akasaka Park Building, 2-3-4 Akasaka, Minato-ku,
TOKYO 107. Tel. 586-2016

KOREA – CORÉE
Pan Korea Book Corporation,
P.O.Box n° 101 Kwangwhamun, SÉOUL. Tel. 72-7369

LEBANON – LIBAN
Documenta Scientifica/Redico,
Edison Building, Bliss Street, P.O.Box 5641, BEIRUT.
Tel. 354429–344425

MALAYSIA – MALAISIE
and/et SINGAPORE-SINGAPOUR
University of Malaya Co-operative Bookshop Ltd.
P.O. Box 1127, Jalan Pantai Baru
KUALA LUMPUR Tel. 51425, 54058, 54361

THE NETHERLANDS – PAYS-BAS
Staatsuitgeverij
Verzendboekhandel
Chr. Plantijnstraat
'S-GRAVENHAGE   Tel. nr. 070-789911
Voor bestellingen: Tel. 070-789208

NEW ZEALAND – NOUVELLE-ZÉLANDE
The Publications Manager,
Government Printing Office,
WELLINGTON: Mulgrave Street (Private Bag),
World Trade Centre, Cubacade, Cuba Street,
Rutherford House, Lambton Quay, Tel. 737-320
AUCKLAND: Rutland Street (P.O.Box 5344), Tel. 32.919
CHRISTCHURCH: 130 Oxford Tce (Private Bag), Tel. 50.331
HAMILTON: Barton Street (P.O.Box 857), Tel. 80.103
DUNEDIN: T & G Building, Princes Street (P.O.Box 1104),
Tel. 78.294

NORWAY – NORVÈGE
J.G. TANUM A/S
P.O. Box 1177 Sentrum
Karl Johansgate 43
OSLO 1   Tel (02) 80 12 60

PAKISTAN
Mirza Book Agency, 65 Shahrah Quaid-E-Azam, LAHORE 3.
Tel. 66839

PORTUGAL
Livraria Portugal, Rua do Carmo 70-74,
1117 LISBOA CODEX.
Tel. 360582/3

SPAIN – ESPAGNE
Mundi-Prensa Libros, S.A.
Castellò 37, Apartado 1223, MADRID-1. Tel. 275.46.55
Libreria Bastinos, Pelayo, 52, BARCELONA 1. Tel. 222.06.00

SWEDEN – SUÈDE
AB CE Fritzes Kungl Hovbokhandel,
Box 16 356, S 103 27 STH, Regeringsgatan 12,
DS STOCKHOLM. Tel. 08/23 89 00

SWITZERLAND – SUISSE
Librairie Payot, 6 rue Grenus, 1211 GENÈVE 11. Tel. 022-31.89.50

TAIWAN – FORMOSE
National Book Company,
84-5 Sing Sung South Rd., Sec. 3, TAIPEI 107. Tel. 321.0698

THAILAND – THAILANDE
Suksit Siam Co., Ltd.
1715 Rama IV Rd.
Samyan, Bangkok 5
Tel. 2511630

UNITED KINGDOM – ROYAUME-UNI
H.M. Stationery Office, P.O.B. 569,
LONDON SE1 9 NH. Tel. 01-928-6977, Ext. 410 or
49 High Holborn, LONDON WC1V 6 HB (personal callers)
Branches at: EDINBURGH, BIRMINGHAM, BRISTOL,
MANCHESTER, CARDIFF, BELFAST.

UNITED STATES OF AMERICA – ÉTATS-UNIS
OECD Publications and Information Center, Suite 1207,
1750 Pennsylvania Ave., N.W. WASHINGTON, D.C.20006.
Tel. (202)724-1857

VENEZUELA
Libreria del Este, Avda. F. Miranda 52, Edificio Galipàn,
CARACAS 106. Tel. 32 23 01/33 26 04/33 24 73

YUGOSLAVIA – YOUGOSLAVIE
Jugoslovenska Knjiga, Terazije 27, P.O.B. 36, BEOGRAD.
Tel. 621-992

Les commandes provenant de pays où l'OCDE n'a pas encore désigné de dépositaire peuvent être adressées à :
OCDE, Bureau des Publications, 2 rue André-Pascal, 75775 PARIS CEDEX 16.
Orders and inquiries from countries where sales agents have not yet been appointed may be sent to:
OECD, Publications Office, 2 rue André-Pascal, 75775 PARIS CEDEX 16.

OECD PUBLICATIONS, 2 rue André-Pascal, 75775 PARIS CEDEX 16 – No. 41 423 1980
PRINTED IN FRANCE
(1000 Q- 97 80 04 1) ISBN 92-64-12063-7